TEACHING CONFIDENCE IN THE CLOUDS

AN INSTRUCTOR'S GUIDE TO USING DESKTOP FLIGHT SIMULATORS

What Reviewers Are Saying About
TEACHING CONFIDENCE IN THE CLOUDS

"Desktop training devices have revolutionized the way pilots learn to fly on instruments, and now—at last!—the teaching techniques are addressed in a clear and organized fashion. Bravo for Tom Gilmore! As a NAFI Master Instructor and tireless advocate for professional devotion to the craft, he has created a tool which thousands will call on time and again."

—*Rusty Sachs, NAFI Executive Director*

"Someone needed to write this book, and with his years of instrument-training experience—both in the cockpit and at the instructor console—Tom's shown why he's the guy to do it. In his attempt to show how useful these devices are in everyday instrument training, Tom shoots and scores.

"Tom offers his hard-earned insight into using one of the most useful—but least used—tools in the flight instructor's arsenal, the personal computer-based aviation training device. With his guidance, instructors will learn how to teach the judgment, organization, and discipline students need to fly in today's complex instrument environment."

—*Greg Laslo, Editor, NAFI Mentor*

"Tom offers a convincing argument for the use of desktop simulators in the instrument training syllabus, and then goes on to present numerous tips for their practical use.... a must read for any serious instrument instructor."

—*Doug Stewart, 2004 CFI of the year*

"Master CFI Tom Gilmore has created a text that will aid flight instructors in becoming more efficient, effective aviation educators...This, in turn, should lead to better prepared intrument students who have more money left in their pockets at the end of their training regimens."

—*Sandy and JoAnn Hill, Administrators of the NAFI Master Instructor Program*

TEACHING CONFIDENCE IN THE CLOUDS

AN INSTRUCTOR'S GUIDE TO USING DESKTOP FLIGHT SIMULATORS

Aviation Supplies & Academics, Inc.
Newcastle, Washington

Teaching Confidence in the Clouds:
An instructor's guide to using desktop flight simulators
by Tom Gilmore

Published by
Aviation Supplies & Academics, Inc.
7005 132nd Place SE • Newcastle, WA 98059
(425) 235-1500 • email asas@asa2fly.com
Internet: www.asa2fly.com

Photo/illustration credits and acknowledgements. Page xii, photo courtesy SDASM (San Diego Aerospace Museum) Library and Archives; Page xiii, "Blue Box" photo © L-3 Link Simulation and Training, used by permission; Page 3, 11, courtesy www.brooks.af.mil (website of Air Force Links Photos at Brooks City-Base); Page 4 (left), courtesy Air Force Links Photos; Page 4 (right), courtesy SDASM; Page 5, courtesy Link-Roberson Collection, Special Collections at Binghamton University Libraries; Page 16, courtesy Mark Anders, Lexington, KY; Page 17, courtesy ELITE; Page 18, 20, 24, 26, ©ASA, Inc.; Page 67, from FAA Technical Report (DOT/FAA/AM-02/19, Oct.2002); Page 68 and 69, courtesy Garmin. Photos used by permission—the author and publisher wish to thank the contributors for use of photography. All other photographs are by the author, all illustrations by the author (© Thomas Gilmore).

Printed in the United States of America
10 09 08 07 9 8 7 6 5 4 3 2 1

ASA-PC-SIMS
ISBN 1-56027-681-9
978-1-56027-681-4

Library of Congress Cataloging-in-Publication Data:
Gilmore, Tom
Teaching confidence in the clouds : an instructor's guide to using desktop flight simulators / Tom Gilmore.
p. cm.
Includes bibliographical references and index.
ISBN-13: 978-1-56027-681-4 (pbk.)
ISBN-10: 1-56027-681-9 (pbk.)
1. Flight training--Data processing. 2. Flight simulators. 3. Computer flight games. I. Title.
TL712.8.G55 2007
629.132'52078--dc22

2007010285

CONTENTS

PREFACE

Do you use a computer desktop flight simulator or flight training device (FTD) in your training program as a flight instructor? If not, this book might convince you that desktop flight simulators are a meaningful tool for training students and helping pilots maintain instrument flying proficiency.

This personal computer aviation training device (PCATD) or basic aviation training device (Basic ATD) is a relatively new technology flight instructors and pilots can use to advance their training techniques and increase their skills as pilots. I will refer to this technology as "simulator" throughout this book, even though the FAA placed the PCATD in a separate category following approval in 1997. Since then, the PCATD has proven itself as a valuable teaching tool for ten of the 40 minimum hours of experience required in instrument rating and to polish the skills for even the most experienced pilot. The Basic ATD can be used for ten of the required 40 minimum hours, as well as to meet the 14 CFR §61.57 instrument currency requirements (six instrument approaches, holding procedures, intercepting and tracking NAVAIDs every six months), 2.5 hours towards Private Pilot certification, and one hour of instrument training for the FAA Wings Program.

I have been in the flight training business for almost 40 years and was one of the first flight instructors to make use of the PCATD in my accelerated instrument training program. I have successfully signed off a high number of instrument checkride applicants, proving the usefulness of desktop flight simulation devices in training.

With the rapid development of glass cockpit aircraft, training methods are being modified to make the transition more efficient. The latest scenario-based training concepts have been proven to lower the time a pilot learns to fly the newer technically advanced aircraft (TAA). The FAA, along with many of the industry leaders, has been coordinating this activity. The FAA Industry Training Standards (FITS) and their use for augmenting desktop simulation training are discussed in this book.

This book is not an owner's manual for PCATDs or computer-based flight simulators. Although it focuses on the ASA On Top software and PCATD hardware, the information herein can be applied to most computer flight simulators. The content should be used in addition to manufacturer-provided documentation and other training manuals you might have.

Rather than use "he/she" throughout the text, I have opted to alternate between the two at random. In no case has preference been given to either choice.

I hope you find this book a valuable resource that provides guidance for your training endeavors as you use a desktop flight simulator.

INTRODUCTION

We have entered into a new and challenging era regarding the training of general aviation pilots. Innovative aircraft design and recent advances in avionics technology have forced pilots to change how they use and pilot their aircraft. This has made it mandatory for the active flight instructor to adopt new skills and develop creative training methods for teaching pilots to fly on instruments.

Flight instructors have historically relied on teaching aids to reinforce the learning process. Small model aircraft with movable flight controls, sketching flight maneuvers on a pad of paper, or using hand motions were some of the early basic tools used by flight instructors. Crude and inefficient as these methods were, they still aided the transfer of knowledge from flight instructor to the student. In a pinch, these training aides are still used today, especially in the confines of the "smallest classroom in the world"—the aircraft cockpit.

Today, however, we have a more efficient training tool at our disposal. This tool is the desktop flight simulator software, or, when combined with hardware controls, a Personal Computer-Based Aviation Training Device, or PCATD. The PCATD is not recognized as a flight simulator by the FAA. I will describe four levels of computer simulation devices covered in the following chapters, but for the sake of simplicity, I will use the term "simulator" when discussing all of them in this book. The desktop flight simulator PCATD is in a class all by itself, but the average pilot can still consider it a flight simulator.

This book is designed to provide flight instructors with the information they need to effectively use computer desktop flight simulators and flight training devices, although it is not limited to their use. It includes advice and lessons I have learned from teaching instrument pilots around the country.

This manual would not be complete without some history of instrument flight. The pioneers of aviation discovered early on that spatial disorientation would prove to be a large obstacle in making flight a practical form of transportation. A number of inventive geniuses made it all possible, and their stories leading up to the modern day desktop simulation devices are quite fascinating.

The year 1929 was a high tech time in history for instrument flying developments. Jimmy Doolittle made his historic blind takeoff and landing, while Lawrence "Gyro" Sperry was busy developing the gyroscopic flight instruments. William Charles Ocker, who was considered the "father of blind flying," was writing the first training manual for instrument flight titled *Blind Flight in Theory and Practice*, which was first published in 1930. Final publication was in 1932.

Lawrence "Gyro" Sperry

In 1929, Edwin A. Link also patented the first true instrument flight simulator. The Link Trainer, as it was called, was a

Link's Blue Box

full-motion simulator derived from a vacuum-operated organ. It was sold to the military for training both Army Air Corps and airmail pilots to fly on instruments. Affectionately dubbed "the Blue Box," it provided many early pilots with the necessary discipline and training to trust their aircraft flight instruments when entering the clouds. Without the concerted effort of these smart and progressive visionaries, instrument flight would not have been possible.

Hood time in a pilot's logbook during the early years of instrument training was truly that—a large canvas hood was pulled over the cockpit of the training pilot. The flight instructor or safety pilot normally sat in front of the student and could see outside the aircraft to avoid collision with either the ground or other aircraft. The training pilot could not see outside the aircraft, and if he lost control of the aircraft while flying on pure instruments, the unhooded instructor could then take over control. The foggles and flip-up hood designs of today are a far cry from the canvas hoods of the past.

After the Link Trainer, more advanced simulators were produced. Some had full motion, while others were stationary enclosures that provided proof that motion was not a necessary requirement in producing a basic instrument flight simulator. Several companies were producing flight simulator hardware that met the needs of the general aviation pilot, but at a cost that only larger flight schools were able to afford.

In the 1970s, a desktop flight trainer was developed and sold by a company called ATC. The first model sold was the ATC-510 and did not have some of the more advanced features of the next version which was the ATC-610. The ATC-610 was the primary hardware unit that was integrated into many accelerated instrument training programs. The proof of concept these flight and ground training programs capitalized on was the use of an approved desktop FTD that lowered the time required in an aircraft to obtain an instrument rating. The FAA approved this device for twenty of the required forty hours minimum flight time needed to qualify for the rating. Many of these units are still in the field and have value, but they are becoming increasingly outdated with the advent of computer simulators.

In the late 1990s, the FAA approved the PCATD, and it has since been instrumental in teaching instrument flying skills to many pilots when properly integrated into a flight and ground training program. Many instrument flight tasks that need to be mastered in an aircraft can be easily introduced through use of a desktop flight simulator.

The success of the PCATD has introduced recent developments in desktop flight simulators. The Basic Aviation Training Device (B-ATD) and the Advanced Aviation Training Device (A-ATD) have come into production. Both of these desktop simulator units have been approved by the FAA to provide logbook credit for all of the six approaches and holds required in 14 CFR §61.57(c) for the six month currency. This added endorsement by the FAA has lowered the warning flags initially raised by early doomsayers of PCATD desktop training. A good percentage of the instrument-rated pilots flying in today's airspace have had some exposure to the PCATD or desktop simulator training.

"The smallest classroom in the world."

Not only have these high tech flight simulation devices provided a more effective way to teach flight students to fly on instruments, but they have also changed the methods used for teaching. The modern glass cockpit aircraft is more complex and presents additional teaching challenges to the modern-day flight instructor. New FAA Industry Training Standards (FITS) were jointly developed by the FAA and the GA community to make this teaching challenge less formidable. This book covers the methods flight instructors can learn to use the newer scenario-based teaching techniques in their flight training programs.

How to effectively use the computer desktop flight simulators in training is the primary focus of this book. I will explain in detail how I use the On Top PCATD in my instrument training program. I have described some of my more interesting training assignments and instructor tips in hopes they will reduce the time needed to complete an instrument training program.

The advantages gained by using desktop flight simulators in instrument training are more obvious today than ever before. No fuel is burned and precious time is not lost to get vectored back for another approach. Desktop simulator training is a more relaxed training environment, and weather is not a barrier to getting valuable training.

So strap in! I am taking you for an instructional ride into the world of virtual flight. It is a fascinating and worthwhile adventure. Teaching a student to fly in the clouds with confidence is one of the most rewarding endeavors you will ever receive as an instructor, and the training you provide will make it a reality.

1

THE HISTORY OF INSTRUMENT FLIGHT

...Without their joint efforts, instrument flight and the practical use of aircraft for transportation might not have been possible.

THE EARLY PIONEERS

Let's step back about 80 years and look at the progress that's been made in instrument flight. History tells us many interesting stories about the people who led the charge toward learning to fly on the gauges. These stories are the springboard for all the expertise leading up to our current glass cockpit technology.

The early pilots realized the aeroplane was a great traveling machine, but it lacked the equipment that could take it to a practical level. The Wright Brothers had set the stage with their first recorded powered flight in 1903. Aircraft design, along with brave pilots making trial and error flights, was moving the field of aviation toward a new frontier, marked by what seemed like an impossible feat: true instrument flight.

Pilots and aircraft manufacturers were already pushing the limits of flying cross-country in good weather. It was when they lost sight of the ground that their feelings of safety began to fade. It must have been an exciting time in aviation as the mysteries of instrument flying were unraveled. The first fledgling pilots who tried trusting their inner senses would have met with horror as they spiraled out of the overcast skies. Most did not survive.

Four pioneers rose to the challenge of solving the complex environment associated with instrument flight and combined their talents during the late 1920s. They were William Charles Ocker, Jimmy Doolittle, Lawrence Sperry and Edwin Link. Without their joint efforts, instrument flight and the practical use of aircraft for transportation might not have been possible.

Back then, instrument flying was a mystery. Spatial disorientation (SD) as we know it today was not a known human frailty. The first discovery of spatial disorientation was made when a heavier-than-air aircraft entered a cloud. A young Dutch pilot at RNAF Soesterberg noticed the earth's horizon was tilted upon exiting a cloud formation in his vintage WWI aircraft, although he had the perception of flying straight and level inside the clouds.

William Charles Ocker

William Ocker held the rank of Corporal when he proposed the theory that pilots shared a weakness in not knowing which end was up without external references. He was a Colonel by the time he completed his research. Most of his contribution to instrument flight came prior to the invention of the artificial horizon and directional gyro. When Ocker discovered and experimented with SD, the turn and bank indicator was the only gyro instrument that could be counted on for maintaining level flight in the clouds. Because of this, Ocker was the first person to dispel the idea that a pilot could keep an aircraft in controlled flight in the clouds simply by feel. This "seat of the pants" method of instrument flying managed to kill a lot of pilots, especially airmail pilots. Before long, these accidents got the government's attention, which led to an all out effort to solve the problem. Eventually, pilots understood that the ear's vestibular system could not keep a pilot in control when flying without the natural horizon.

Ocker and his assistant, Carl J. Crane, experimented with an early training simulator, and Ocker wrote the world's first manual for instrument flight, *Blind Flight in Theory and Practice* (1932). Orville Wright once called Ocker a great "missionary" for instrument flying and credited him with having the most influence on the study of instrument flight training.

William Ocker

Ocker and Crane performed some unpredictable experiments, such as dumping blindfolded pigeons from aloft. After spiraling around and flying upside-down, the pigeons just spread their wings and floated safely to earth. The two investigators were thus convinced of ways to overcome spatial disorientation without reference to outside cues. We, of course, know that what gave the blindfolded pigeons a safe descent to earth is not what pilots use to confidently fly on instruments.

Colonel Ocker's solution was to configure the turn and bank indicator, the airspeed indicator and the compass. These primary instruments helped the pilot determine his correct orientation regardless of outside conditions. Colonel Ocker, along with Lieutenant Crane, began to train Brooks' air base cadets in the use of instrument flying techniques. To demonstrate the effectiveness of instrument flying, Colonel Ocker flew 900 miles, solely by instrument reference, from Brooks Field to Scott Field in 1930. Shortly after, the military began experimenting with his innovative system and by the outset of World War II, instrument flying was a solid element of aircraft design and pilot training.

Prior to the invention of the gyro horizon, when the turn and bank indicator was the only gyro instrument available, flight instructors had developed a 1-2-3 system to train their pilots. The 1-2-3 system was also known as flying by "needle-ball and airspeed." When a pilot got caught in instrument conditions, this system could be used as a last resort and did save lives. An early training publication incorrectly stated that "a pilot should keep the ball centered with ailerons and the needle centered with rudder." Pilots, through trial and error, however, correctly found that the needle should be centered with the ailerons and the ball should be centered with the rudder. Fortunately, the old manual didn't stay in publication long because the gyro horizon was brought into full production and most pilots were getting trained to the new "attitude system" of flying during World War II.

Here is how the old manual read as an *incorrect* procedure:

1. Use only the rudder to center the needle.
2. Use only the ailerons to center the ball.
3. Use only the elevator to maintain the proper airspeed.

Many pilots realized that engine power also played a big role in the recovery technique to regain altitude, so they added throttle as an extra step to the 1-2-3 system.

Jimmy Doolittle and Lawrence Sperry

In the next phase in the evolution of instrument flying, Jimmy Doolittle and Lawrence Sperry combined their inventive talents to design the gyro horizon and gyro compass or directional gyro. Doolittle was the test pilot for many flights that led up to his first blind takeoff and landing. This historic flight took place on September 24, 1929 in a NY-2 Husky Biplane.

Later in his life, Doolittle said he made hundreds of practice flights before making his milestone "blind" flight. He admitted that the final blind takeoff and landing made in 1929 was his most important contribution to aviation. It is an amazing statement considering Doolittle made the famous Tokyo raid over Japan. Though considered a failure in some ways, the raid was instrumental in raising the morale of our country during WWII.

Jimmy Doolittle and Lawrence Sperry.

Doolittle proved that an aircraft could take off and land with no outside reference, but Sperry's invention was the key to making it happen. Doolittle's flight was also made feasible by the introduction of the sensitive altimeter. Without it, his "soft landing" to mother earth would not have been achievable. Looking back, his 15-minute flight would become one of the most historic aviation events of the century.

It is interesting to note that Doolittle was enclosed in a hooded cockpit in the rear of the tandem aircraft. His safety pilot was Second Lieutenant Kelsey. The Daniel Guggenheim Fund for Safety in Aviation was the sponsor of the event. The foundation had developed a fog dispersal apparatus that allowed pilots to fly during horrendous flight conditions. According to Doolittle, it was zero-zero! This made the takeoff truly dicey, even with Kelsey flying up front. Thirteen minutes later, during the landing, the fog had risen enough so that Doolittle could have made a landing without any instruments, but he did it under the hood. Kelsey must have been extremely thankful he could see the ground when they floated from the clouds.

According to stories told by pioneer pilots who were trained in the blind landing technique, the blind landing experimental planes were guided by two low-frequency radio beacons positioned along the final approach path to the turf landing area. After lining up with the two beacons and crossing the innermost beacon at a prescribed altitude, the aircraft had to be kept level while the pilot stayed straight on track with the directional gyro. Then, the pilot could slowly let down, maintaining a predetermined speed and descent rate, until the main wheels hit the turf. As instrument pilots and instructors, we can greatly appreciate the courage it must have taken to perform these blind landings, whether the landing area was a wide pasture or a runway.

The proven success and acceptance of the gyro horizon meant many pilots would need a training regimen that could provide the discipline needed to fly on instruments. It had to be a mass training program because the U.S. was just entering WWII.

Edwin Link

A young self-taught engineer, Edwin Link, was already working out the solution to instrument training obstacles with the invention of his "Blue Box" flight simulator. Of the four pioneer pilots, Ed Link's life is the most interesting to certified instrument flight instructors (CFII) and those of us who use flight simulators today.

Edwin Link.

Link was a real visionary who loved aviation, but he knew the limits of flying aircraft into poor weather without instrument training. His family business produced bellows-driven organs and gave him the background to engineer a crude instrument flight simulator.

Attempts to simulate flight were made even before Link successfully did so with his trainer. Two of the first attempts were billed as "The Sanders' Teacher" and "The Early-Billing Oscillator." The Wright Brothers had even tried to build a crude flight simulator by cutting up an old damaged cockpit and mounting it on sawhorses. All of these early efforts produced flight simulators, but none could compare to the Link.

Early pilots used a system they referred to as the "Penguin System," which was developed by the French. Instructors allowed the would-be pilots to get the feel of the aircraft controls by taxiing around on the ground, which did cut down the flight time required for pilots to earn their wings. Link considered this system when first developing his original trainer in the basement of the organ factory.

Although his first efforts went unnoticed, Link found a small market for his flight simulator and sold 50 units to amusement parks in 1930. Rides were 25 cents each. Only two units went to the aviation industry, without instruments, at a cost of $450 each. On September 29, 1931, a patent was issued to Link for his simulator, which was then called a "Pilot Maker." By this time, his model had a full complement of gyro instrumentation. The official technical description was a "Combination Training Device for Student Aviators and Entertainment Apparatus." The depression years that followed were not a favorable time to market and sell any nonessential mechanical device, especially the Link Trainer, so times were tough for Link.

He and his wife, Marion, operated a flight school in Binghamton, New York. He started documenting instructional procedures as he taught his students to fly. From this hodgepodge of paperwork, his wife organized the papers into a formal manuscript that became one of the first documented simulator training publications. It was designed to supplement the flying school and train his students in his new invention, the flightless airplane.

Link made improvements that added options and sophistication to the Link Simulator, which caused some seasoned and well-known pilots to realize the value of his invention. One of his first major sales contracts was with Charles S. (Casey) Jones, one of the first and most noted pilots of the time. (He was officially issued the 13th pilot's license.) He bought six of the trainers for his flight school and contracted with Link to do the training.

The little invention that was probably considered too high tech for its time lingered in obscurity until Casey arranged to have Link meet with military representatives in New Jersey. Because of Link's reputation, the meeting generated much interest in the "Blue Box" trainer. Some newspapers and periodicals published reports that said by blind flying on the trainer, one could shorten essential air training by more than 50%.

On February 11, 1934, Link was scheduled to fly some 200 miles from Binghamton to Newark to demonstrate his simulator to a group of Air Corps representatives. The Army Air Corp had taken over flying the mail and had experienced a rash of fatal crashes, which stirred the need for the simulator.

It was a dismal and foggy day when Link took off from the Binghamton Airport. While the Air Corps representatives and Jones were waiting in the nasty weather in Newark, they speculated that Link would have to turn back. As they were preparing to leave, they heard the faint drone of an aircraft engine. "He had made it on instruments," wrote one biographer. After his perfect landing out of the clouds, orders began pouring into the Link production plant from the government. Link's little "Blue Box" flight simulator had finally made it to the big time.

By 1936, the Model "A" simulator was equipped with a compass, airspeed indicator, rate-of-climb and turn-and-bank indicators, volume control for the pilot within a pre-selected range, and instruments that allowed an instructor to transmit simulated radio signals to a student during practice. The Model "B" was a more advanced version of the Model "A" with the Model "C" soon to follow. The Model "C" was the most sophisticated of the Link models and featured a full-scale instrument panel and desk assembly for an instructor. The Model "D" was then produced to satisfy the needs of the European Air Force. Over time, thousands of Links were sold throughout the world.

Link training facilities were set up all over the country to train both military and commercial pilots. Many of the instructors were women, who had accomplished the same training and skills as their male classmates. In fact they had proven themselves to be some of the best instrument pilots and instructors employed by Link. Many were Women Air Force Service Pilots (WASPs) with previous Link experience, so they breezed through military instrument training. Both Pan Am and American Airlines were using Links in their pilot training programs, and they mostly employed women to teach their pilots. The benefits were obvious in both cost and efficiency. Over half a million military pilots were trained with Link trainers during World War II.

After the war, Ed Link had less influence on the design of his highly-sophisticated invention and slowly retired from the company operation. The rest of his life is the topic of many books, as he went on to develop and invent undersea diving vehicles, many which are in use today. He was one of the most important figures of his time, and his legacy lives on today at the Harbor Branch Oceanographic Facility in Ft. Pierce, Florida.

Outside view of "blue box" trainer.

Inside view of "blue box" trainer.

The importance of ground trainers for general aviation did not go unnoticed by Link manufacturing. The old C-8 and C-11 trainers the military had been discarding were now being used as basic trainers in many flight schools. Many older pilots actively flying today will admit to some Link time in their old logbooks. It was a hard sell to get flight instructors of the time to realize the value of the old

Link. They wanted to get their air time, and the schools made more money on aircraft rental, but the "Blue Box" was still a valuable tool for instrument flight instructors.

Link trainers became more sophisticated, and eventually Link was one of two major companies producing flight simulators. At the time, Curtiss-Wright was the only other comparable competitor. Link eventually made the first military jet simulator and produced simulators for the airlines that replicated all the commercial jet aircraft of the time. The first airline to make use of the Link was American Airlines with the first order placed on January 6, 1937—a Model "C." Ultimately a Link simulator was made to duplicate the unique flight characteristics of the SR-71 Blackbird.

The Link Company changed hands several times by merging into major manufacturing firms. Rights were sold to companies who then wanted to diversify the operation. One of these was the Singer Sewing Machine Company. Singer produced a no-motion simulator called the General Aviation Trainer (GAT), which they began selling in 1960. It was mildly successful with flight schools in the 1960s and early 1970s, but the cost was high.

DEVELOPMENT OF THE AIRWAY SYSTEM

A more in-depth look into history will show that air navigation was the last phase of air travel that needed to be conquered so the airplane could be considered a practical form of transportation. Early pilots tried various methods to stay in ground contact. This meant they had to hedgehop their way across the country to stay on course. The first cross-country pioneer pilots used a system they called Contact Flight Rules (CFR).

Even before flights were being made on instruments, there was an airway system. During the day, pilots used known checkpoints to navigate their way across the country. At night they used a series of lights or beacons across the middle section of the country, from New York to California. The middle 1,000 miles had to be illuminated so they could fly it by night. The early pilots, flying in good weather, could get away with a minimum of one light every 100 miles. But the moment the weather got hazy, no matter how bright the light was, they couldn't see it from 100 miles away. Consequently, they had to have another beacon called the intermediate field beacon, which was placed every 10 miles. It was an incandescent lamp mounted in an 18-inch reflector on the top of a tower. The larger 100-mile beacons marked the location of airports. Many of these beacons used the tops of windmills, which were common during the 1920s and 1930s.

The next airway system was the Adcock or Loop radio range that transmitted low frequency transmission in the 200–500 kilocycle frequency range. These stations were positioned every 75–100 miles to form an airway system across the country.

The radio signal was transmitted in four steady-tone narrow quadrants that could be flown to and from the station. If a pilot got off the beam, they heard either an A (• —) or an N (— •). When pilots were on the "beam," they heard a steady tone in their headset. The alignment of the beam put the pilot on a known path over the ground. The stations provided the first crude form of instrument approach to airports and had call letters so they could be identified for navigation. All stations had three letter alpha characters for Morse code identification.

Once an airway system was implemented, there was no stopping full-service instrument flight in the United States. Pilots could now have faith in their instrument panel guiding the way with or without reference to land.

INSTRUMENT VIEW LIMITING DEVICES

How do you build a better mousetrap? That has been a question plaguing pilots from the first time they started using view-limiting devices in the cockpit. Instructors and inventive entrepreneurs have tried to devise different ways to block the pilot's view of outside without affecting the view of the safety pilot.

It all began with perhaps the most effective technique, the canvas hood. The column heading "hood" used in many logbooks can be traced back to the early days of instrument flight training. The original hood covered up an entire single-place cockpit. There was absolutely no way to peek outside of the aircraft, so the first pilots who logged instrument time were completely on the gauges.

When Jimmy Doolittle made his famous blind takeoff and landing on September 24, 1929, he used the full hood. He sat covered in the rear seat of a tandem cockpit while the observer sat in the front, making sure he didn't fly into something. "Blind flight" was the early term used to describe flight without the natural horizon. Later the expression "instrument flight" was coined to describe flying with total reliance on the gyros. The date when instrument flight became the official technical jargon cannot be verified. It is probably safe to assume this happened when the first instrument-rated pilots were launched into the system. Today, most newly-rated instrument pilots receive very little actual instrument meteorological conditions (IMC) training during their initial instrument training. Therefore, every instrument instructor knows how important it is to keep students from looking outside while logging instrument time.

After WWII, as side-by-side cockpits replaced tandem seating aircraft, flight instructors covered the left side of the cockpit with sections of canvas. This was a primitive, if unsafe, solution to the automotive-style seating in aircraft design. The instructor was totally blocked from seeing any threatening traffic on the student's side of the aircraft, yet it was the accepted method of teaching instrument pilots. The big sky/little airplane principle made in-flight collisions a remote possibility.

Hooded student in military side-by-side aircraft.

Today, for the sake of quality training, an instructor must understand the limitations of commonly used hoods and incorporate real-world IMC flying into the curriculum as much as possible. The problem with many current view restrictors is that they are less effective, and students are getting cheated by too much "information" from the outside world. This can be seen with students the first time we fly into actual IMC—even after hours of flying under the hood. They start to drift off heading and altitude almost immediately.

We've all seen the flip-up/flip-down plastic visor. The convenience of these fitting over glasses makes them a choice for many pilots and instructors, although the FAA originally questioned their ability to adequately restrict the outside view. But after weighing the increased safety benefits, they allowed their use. In spite of their popularity, they blocked the instructor's traffic scan between the nine and eleven o'clock position and were proven to have caused several catastrophic mid-air collisions.

Some instructors are resistant to using view-limiting devices, stating they have limited training value. Some are so convinced of their uselessness that they do most of their training with instrument students in actual IMC. Unfortunately, this is not always practical.

One instructor, who started his instrument instruction in the mid 1950s, claimed he used a Stinson 108 that was equipped with an amber-colored plastic film to selectively cover the inside windows. The film was cut to fit and taped to the windshield and side windows.

When flying on a clear and cloudless day, vision was excellent with only an amber tint on the windows for both student and instructor. He then put a blue wrap around the student's goggles. If the student looked outside, he saw total blackness, and inside he saw the instrument panel clearly, but with a slightly blue tint. Apparently this vision-limiting technique was used by other flight schools and even the airlines for a short time. Perhaps it could be revived as a more effective instrument flight rules (IFR) training tool. In fact when the FAA conducted a study on the loss of primary flight instruments in October 2002 (read report in Chapter 7), it used a similar material to block the outside view of the 41 pilots being tested.

There are other view-limiting options as well. Some creative CFI-Is, realizing they forgot a hood or eyeglass adaption, have made a view-limiting device from a sectional chart. They fold the chart into quarters and slip it under the headset band. Of course, this should be considered a temporary solution. In the meantime, maybe that better mouse-trap is coming!

2

THE HISTORY OF DESKTOP FLIGHT SIMULATORS

. . . This evidence has provided the further acceptance by the FAA for the next generation of PC desktop trainers: the BATD and A-ATD.

MOTION IS NOT A CRUCIAL ELEMENT IN FLIGHT SIMULATION

I am prefacing this chapter with another mention of Ed Link, because he was adamantly opposed to any flight simulator that did not produce motion. There were many heated discussions in meetings between Link and his designers about the need to produce motion in a simulator in order to accurately reflect the true fidelity of an aircraft. When he left the company, his feelings and opinions went with him. He might have been a true genius and great visionary, but research following his famous Pilot Trainer has proven that motion is not a crucial component for producing quality flight simulation. Hence, many of today's flight training devices (FTD) do not use motion in their design; the desktop flight simulator is no exception.

The mind can be tricked into believing there is motion without the body actually moving. Try to visualize the following situation: you are in a parked car or stationary boat. You raise your head quickly and see another car or boat slowly pass parallel to your position. For a moment, it is easy to believe you are moving, not the car or boat.

Motion, therefore, can be simulated without actually being produced. When I am training an instrument student that is "flying" a desktop flight simulator, they will sometimes lean in a turn or lift up or down as they notice a change in the attitude indicator.

The first real approved desktop flight simulator.

To give the old ATC-610 credit, it was the first low-cost desktop FTD that provided credibility and received the FAA's blessing for logging instrument time. In fact it started a revolution back in 1970 when the first model, the ATC-510, made it out of production, selling for under $1,000.

At the time, I owned and operated a 141 FAA-approved flight school in Detroit, MI and was one of the first "guinea pig" purchasers of those new fandangled units. It was such a novelty at the time, and I was asked to appear on a local TV show to demonstrate how it was used in my school. My GI trainees were eating up time on this new training tool, and what the ATC-510 lacked in looks, it made up for in features. Following on the heels of the ATC-510 came the ATC-610, an improved version with advanced features. Until the approval of the first PCATD, the ATC-610 was considered the primary instrument training desktop simulator in the field. When I joined Professional Instrument Courses, Inc. (PIC) in 1996 this was the cornerstone of their accelerated training program.

The ATC-610 took a real beating during shipment to various locations throughout the country for the PIC training assignments, so the manufacturer designed a custom hard-shell protective cover to contain them. Often, they arrived with parts rattling around after having been dropped from delivery trucks. A panic call to the PIC headquarters in Essex, CT usually resulted in parts being shipped overnight to field repair the damaged unit. I had a lot of respect for the abuse these little wonder boxes withstood, and they did serve their purpose well. Even when the weather was below minimums, I could do a lot of valuable preparation with my students using the desktop ATC-610 FTD.

Several years later, when I left PIC to develop my own instrument training program using the PCATD, Professional Instrument Courses was still using the ATC-610. In fact, as I write this book, PIC still advertises using the ATC-610, primarily because it is still approved for 20 of the required 40 hours of instrument time. Much credit can therefore be handed to stationary desktop simulators, even before the PCATD appeared on the scene in the late 1990s.

SIMULATION DEVICES

The FAA has made a clear distinction between the three most frequently used simulation devices: the flight simulator, the flight training device (FTD), and the personal computer-based aviation training device (PCATD). They each have different capabilities and are approved to specific qualified levels of use.

The FAA published an Advanced Simulation Plan in 1980, which made flight simulation an operational reality. The plan described three major sets of criteria for determining different levels of training. The criteria encompassed five types of simulators; non-visual, visual, Phase I, Phase II, and Phase III, each which described a level of simulator realism that was progressively more demanding. These standards are still in effect today.

Flight Simulator

14 CFR Part 121 describes a flight simulator as "a full-size aircraft cockpit replica of a specific type of aircraft, or make, model, and series of aircraft, which includes the hardware and software necessary to represent the aircraft in ground operations and flight operations, uses a force cueing system that provides cues at least equivalent to those cues provided by a three-degree freedom of motion system, uses a visual system that provides at least a 45-degree horizontal field of view and a 30-degree vertical field of view simultaneously for each pilot, and has been evaluated, qualified, and approved by the Administrator."

Under AC 120-40, each simulator must represent a specific airplane type and have a motion system. Simulators are designated as Levels A, B, C, and D, and are used extensively for both general aviation and air carrier training and checking in accordance with provisions stated throughout Parts 61, 121, 135, 141, and 142. A pilot can complete total certification and training in a properly-approved simulator and never log one hour in the actual aircraft.

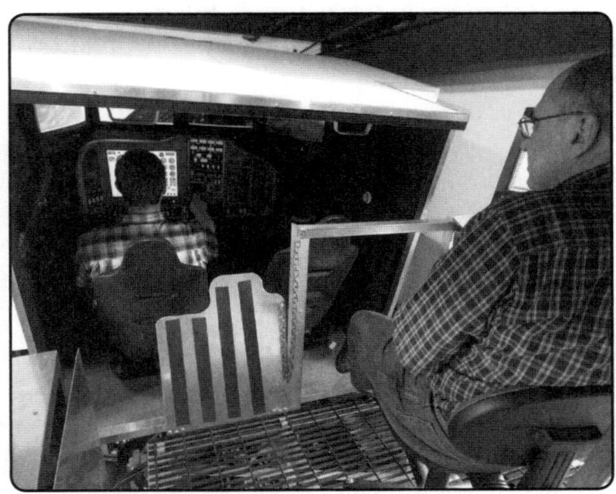

Full-motion simulator.

Flight Training Device (FTD)

FTDs are approved through a process outlined in Advisory Circular (AC) 120-45A. There are six levels of FTDs. Level 1 encompasses ground training devices (GTD). The original Level 1 FTDs are grandfathered under Level 1 until the FAA determines otherwise. This regulation can be found in 14 CFR §61.4(b).

Training hour credit is granted for the six FTD levels based on the maneuvers and procedures authorized under an approved training program. There is an FAA letter of authorization (LOA) for these devices that outlines those specific maneuvers, procedures, or crewmember functions.

FTDs are widely used by both general aviation and air carrier training operations. One of the largest producers of FTDs is Frasca.

View from the cockpit of a Flight Training Device (FTD).

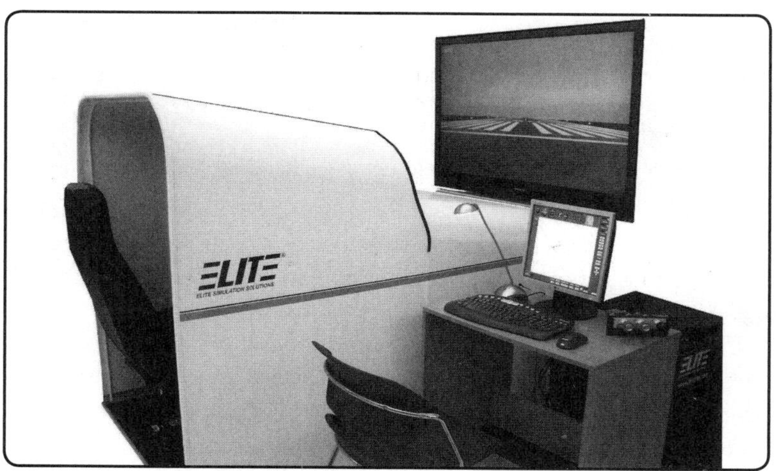

An Elite non-motion FTD.

Personal Computer-Based Aviation Training Devices (PCATD)

Basic computer simulation packages that led to the development of the PCATD appeared over 20 years ago. The FAA eventually acknowledged the merits of computer simulation devices after several studies. In 1997 the PCATD was finally approved for use in a limited training format. AC 61-126 spelled out the guidelines for approval ("Qualification and Approval of Personal Computer-Based Aviation Training Devices").

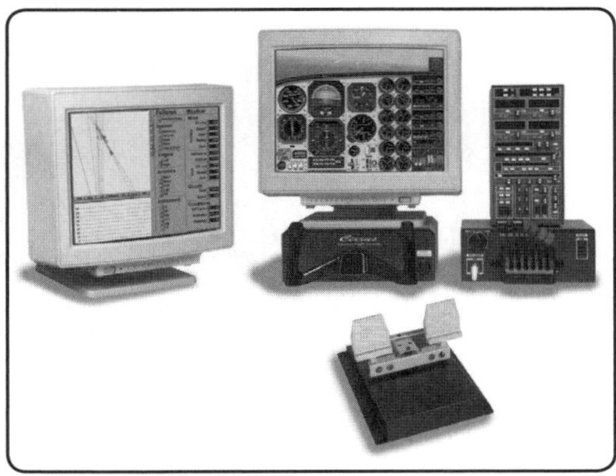

On Top PCATD hardware.

PCATD APPROVAL

In May 1997, the FAA issued AC 61-126 approving the use of PCATDs. The approval granted ten hours of credit for the 40 hours required for an instrument rating. For years, groups like the Aircraft Owners and Pilots Association (AOPA) had supported this technology, so the announcement was a long time coming.

To evaluate the technology, the FAA relied on an extensive research report conducted and submitted by the General Accounting Office (GAO). The report was titled "Research Supports Limited Use of Personal Computer Aviation Training Devices for Pilots." It can be read in its entirety by referencing GAO/RCED-99-143 on the U.S. Government GAO website.

The FAA spent over six years sifting through data collected from two major research projects before making a final decision. The report mentions that the approval sparked debate. Some experts asserted that pilots trained on PCATDs would be less skilled, thereby compromising aviation safety. Others argued that pilots trained with the devices would actually be better trained at a lower cost.

The report went on to define the need for improved training devices with the statistical fact that in 1998, general aviation had 1,907 accidents and 621 fatalities. The National Transportation Safety Board (NTSB) estimated that 87 percent of all fatal general aviation accidents were caused by pilot error, and that pilots without appropriate instrument training were particularly at risk when flying in poor weather. Looking back to the 1930s, the situation is reminiscent of what got the government interested in contracting with Ed Link to sell his first crude "Pilot Maker." In 1998 a low cost, high tech training solution was being sought by the FAA. The PCATD was considered a possible solution.

If you read anything into the FAA's decision to allow ten hours credit toward the initial instrument rating, you would conclude they were just "dipping their toes" in the water to test the outcome of their ruling. One section of the AC encourages PCATD users to submit the name and success rate of any student who trained using the PCATD. Since AC 61-126 was published, reports have favored its continued use. This evidence of the effectiveness of PCATDs has provided the further acceptance by the FAA for the next generation of PC desktop trainers now in production: the Basic ATD (BATD) and the Advanced ATD (AATD).

The PCATD's approval brought about a new class of simulation device. They are not considered either an FTD or flight simulator. Systems that now fall in the flight simulator category require more sophistication, such as the ability to produce more-or-less true motion. No G forces are necessarily experienced as would be in an aircraft, but a fully classified flight simulator provides at least basic flight motion.

BASIC ATD AND ADVANCED ATD APPROVAL

In 2004, the FAA began approving the logging of hours in two newly-classified flight training devices.

The first, a Basic ATD or Basic Aviation Training Device, can be used to perform the following:

1. In addition to the ten hours of instructional use already sanctioned on the PCATD systems, the BATD can be used to perform the approaches, holding procedures, and the intercepting/tracking procedures required under §61.57(c)(1) for recent instrument experience (instrument currency).
2. The BATD devices can also be used to log 2.5 hours toward the Private Pilot License as described under §61.109(i)(1).

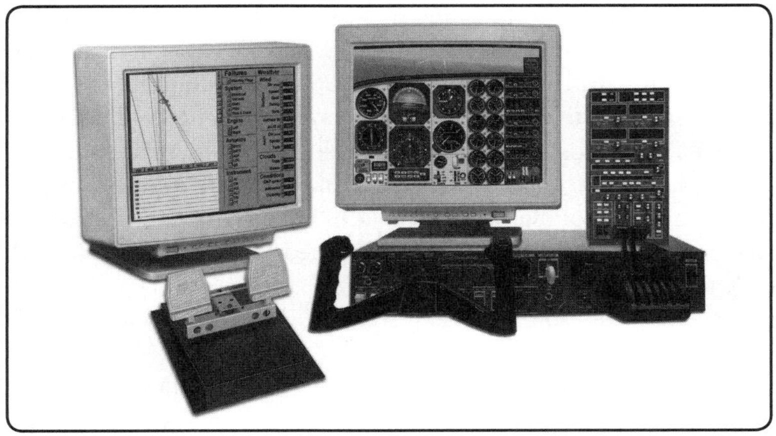

Basic ATD.

The second, a more complex and costly Advanced ATD or Advanced Aviation Training Device can be use to perform the following:

1. Logged flight experience per §61.51(b)(3), i.e., simulated instrument conditions in flight, a flight simulator, or a flight training device.
2. Instrument Experience per §61.57(c)(1), i.e., instrument currency experience.
3. Instrument Proficiency Check per §61.57(d)(1)(ii), i.e., satisfies option to substitute training device for aircraft that can be used for an IPC.
4. Instrument Rating: Practical Test per §61.65.(a)(8), i.e., satisfies option to supplement training device for aircraft that can be used for practical test.
5. Instrument Rating; maximum 20 hours per §61.65(e)(2), i.e., can be used for all 20 of the required 40 hours for the initial instrument rating instead of only 10.
6. Private Pilot Certificate: maximum 2.5 hours per §61.109(i)(1), i.e., same as BATD.
7. Commercial Certificate: maximum 5.0 hours per §61.129(i)(1), i.e., satisfies option to substitute training device for aircraft that can be used for instrument training.
8. Airline Transport Pilot Certificate: maximum 25 hours per §61.159(a)(3)(i), i.e., satisfies option to substitute training device for aircraft that can be used for instrument training.

PCATD INSTRUMENT-TRAINED PILOTS FLY THE SKIES OF TODAY

So far, there is no clear evidence that pilots trained with PCATDs are any less qualified than traditionally trained instrument pilots. In fact, general aviation aircraft accident figures have declined the past seven years since the PCATD was given approval status. There are other factors that come into play, but no evidence can point to any safety issues resulting from the use of a PCATD.

A desktop flight simulator will never handle or respond in the same manner as a real aircraft, but most tasks that must be mastered in the aircraft can be initially taught and practiced by using a PCATD, if it is *integrated* into a flight training program properly. This means that any time spent on a PCATD should be immediately followed by one or two sessions in an aircraft.

An instrument pilot needs to know where she is at any given time and what she will be doing next; it's called situational awareness or positional awareness. Before there were moving map displays, a good instrument pilot needed a fairly accurate mental picture of her position over the ground. It is still a critical and necessary skill, but it only becomes second nature to those who have been trained to develop it. Our current technology has made the average pilot quite lazy in this regard, especially with the cost and availability of new global positioning systems (GPS).

This is one of the main advantages of training with a desktop simulator or PCATD. The training and practice needed for mentally picturing your position can be easily practiced.

Situational awareness is only one of many skills that can be sharpened on a desktop flight simulator. We'll take a look at other skill sets later in the book. Meantime, as we further explore the training medium, keep in mind we are only beginning to scratch the surface of what desktop flight simulation will look like in the future.

DESKTOP SIMULATOR SETUP

*. . . Good flight simulation really comes down to this; the closer we can mimic the reality of flight, the easier it will be to convince training pilots they **might** be flying.*

THE LOCATION AND ENVIRONMENT

The location and surroundings where you set up your simulator are important. You want to be free from outside distractions and away from direct sunlight that can reflect on your PC monitor.

Your choice of monitor, whether cathode-ray tube (CRT) or flat screen, is not important; however it should be at least a 17-inch display, preferably a 19-inch if you can afford it. A CRT monitor has some benefits, such as a wider angle for viewing and true color representation. When used with a full desktop flight simulator setup, the CRT keeps the yoke cabinet from sliding around because of its weight.

As a CFII, you will want a dedicated setup for your desktop simulator. It should be placed in a corner of your office or better yet, a separate room where you'll be free of interruptions to your training sessions. I do not recommend loading additional programs on the computer or using it as a means to access the Internet. Otherwise, your desktop simulator dedicated computer may become infected by a virus or turn into a secondary computer for you, your co-workers or your family to use. I have my PCATD computer totally dedicated to simulator use with my clients. They know this, and it adds one more element of reality to the simulation experience.

In addition to your training station, you may set up your desktop simulator for personal use. It can still have value when installed on your individual PC. With a shortcut icon for your desktop flight simulator software, maintaining instrument proficiency is only a click away. I mention proficiency and not currency, because flying time on any PC simulator in other than PCATD or BATD mode is not loggable.

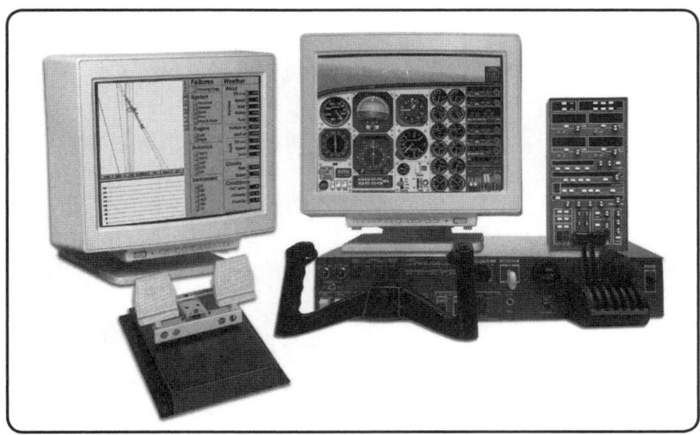

BATD full hardware with instructor station monitor.

PCATD REQUIREMENTS

One strength of the desktop flight simulator is its low cost. Most users would agree that the features they get for the money make the unit more attractive than a high-end machine that costs a fortune.

However, it's important to note you cannot piece one or several of the PCATD or BATD approved hardware/software systems together yourself. Only several manufacturers produce a fully-approved PCATD or BATD that can be used for the initial instrument training. The approved package must not only include the hardware and software, but also a training manual and syllabus. You'll notice in the paperwork that comes with the approved package that the unit is certified only as it was supplied by the manufacturer. In other words the original components must be present to make the entire outfit complete.

To log time on a PCATD or BATD, a certified flight instructor must be present to provide the training. The training must be conducted using a curriculum that incorporates the syllabus that comes with the PCATD or BATD.

The ASA syllabus can be easily incorporated into any training curriculum. In this book I am only going to refer to On Top, as this is the training solution I use with my flight clients. The illustration below shows the complete hardware of yoke, radio stack, rudder pedals and throttle console. The ASA website has details about cost and other options, including the more advanced Basic ATD.

USE A QUALITY TABLE AND CHAIR

A full PCATD setup with all the hardware is hefty, so you need a sturdy, solid table to hold the weight. A good quality chair is also a must, and I highly recommend arm rests; otherwise you or your student/client will quickly tire. The proper height of the table and chair must match the average build of your client base and be adjustable to their needs. I have found office chairs at office supply stores work fine. They provide both height and locking tip adjustment. The chair must remain stationary, especially when you consider the rudder pedals are part of the PCATD hardware requirements. If the chair has roller wheels and is used on a smooth surface such as tile or wood, alter the wheels to keep the chair from sliding away. Whatever your choice of location and furniture, it must be comfortable and meet the needs of the student, or they will acquire a bad taste for flight simulators in general.

A minimal setup for On Top would be a simple joystick plugged into your home PC. This configuration is workable for a typical low cost system. In a pinch, with this basic setup, you can provide a quick lesson to an instrument student. A laptop computer can round off a pretty streamlined training package for travel to and from the airport. It is not a legally logged event, but still can be good for rehearsing an upcoming flight or reviewing what went wrong in the air.

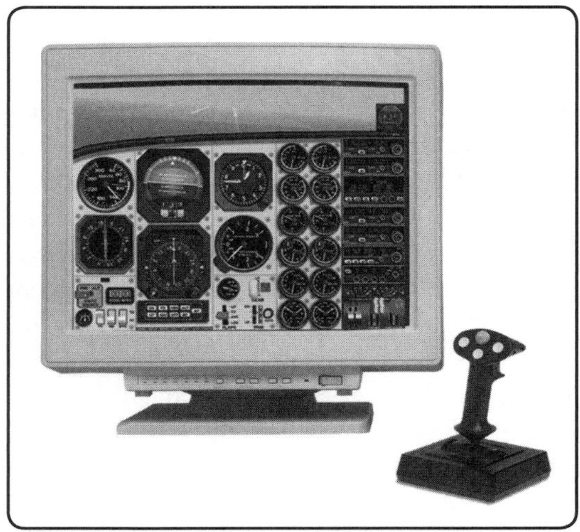

A basic home desktop flight simulator with joystick.

ENCLOSURE NOT NECESSARY

I have trained clients/students using desktop simulators with and without an enclosure. Personally, I do not feel that an enclosure is important to isolate the trainee from outside distractions. Their mind takes over and they soon become engrossed in keeping the instrument needles where they belong, especially if they are scanning properly. The student's peripheral vision soon becomes quite narrow—down to the width of the monitor. No matter what environmental confines are used, a student always knows they are not really flying and that they need to keep their scan up. Some CFIIs have used view-limiting devices during simulation sessions with their students, but in my opinion, they are of limited value unless the trainee specifically requests their use.

On the other hand, the overall physical environment is an important factor. Consider how distracting it would be to use a desktop simulator in the middle of a flight lounge, compared with an enclosed cockpit in a dedicated room. Naturally, the simulated cockpit provides a better training environment, but there are trade-offs in costs and benefits. A quiet undisturbed corner of a room in a comfortable setting works just fine for most desktop training sessions.

When computer simulation software was first developed, it did not provide an accurate depiction of the flight instruments. Because of this, it was extremely hard to convince students they were training in either a flight training device or simulator.

Today's photorealistic panels create a totally different training environment. The choice of different aircraft and the ability to configure instrumentation give students and instructors flexibility that even the big simulators cannot match. The On Top software offers a choice of ten general aviation aircraft models. I recommend you do a custom setup in the beginning of your training sessions to match new students with the aircraft they will be flying (in terms of panel layout). This first step in the setup process provides students with a positive first impression of what the PCATD experience has to offer.

NO DISTRACTIONS, PLEASE!

When giving dual training on a PCATD or other desktop flight simulator, ask your student to turn off their cell phone. Request privacy from other people nearby, and tell your student to clear their mind before you begin the session. Keep the engine sound active in the background as it adds another realistic aspect to the experience. Good flight simulation really comes down to this: the closer you can mimic the reality of flight, the easier it will be to convince training pilots they *might* be flying.

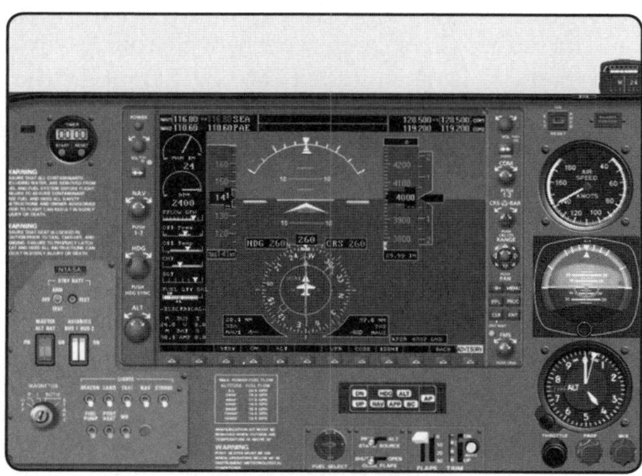

A screen shot of a G1000-like glass cockpit.

CONFIGURING THE ON TOP PCATD

The Avionics Panel: Some of the buttons and knobs are not labeled or are hard to see. Until you've learned what the knobs do, you or your student may have difficulty keeping your scan going while flying the PCATD.

To solve this problem, glue small labels to the buttons and knobs. This helps students become familiar with the avionics panel the first time they sit in front of it without groping through the manual.

The Throttle Quadrant: The throttle quadrant console houses the throttle, propeller and mixture levers as well as the controls for gear, flaps and the rudder trim. The arrangement usually mimics a Piper quadrant in look and feel.

If a multi-engine aircraft is selected, you can exchange the single engine throttle, prop and mixture controls for a multi-engine six-lever quadrant. The first time you do this without the levers in the full aft position, you might be surprised by all the spring force as you loosen the thumb nuts. Remove the single engine quadrant and you will notice six small aluminum rods. These protrude from holes that have springs behind them. These springs cause the resistance when moving the levers.

When exchanging the quadrant hub, move all of the control levers fully aft. This way there will be no force to push the rods out of position when you remove the retaining nuts. It's easy to drop one of the thumb screw nuts, so use caution when doing the exchange with your students.

Yoke and Stand-Alone Throttle: The standard Precision Yoke mimics a Mooney. It has a solid feel and makes good use of two buttons and two rocker switches. On Top buttons can be assigned to different functions, including timer, map screen toggle, pitch trim, and transmit. To configure the yoke in PCATD or BATD mode, the left rocker switch must be assigned to trim up and down, and the right rocker must be assigned to the transmit function. Otherwise, buttons can be selected based on the preference of the operator.

The weight of the yoke control console is heavy for a reason. It makes it difficult to move the yoke console around, especially after you place a 19" monitor on top of it. Pitch is the most prevailing force that could cause movement of the yoke cabinet, but unless a quick and sudden pitch force is applied, it is usually not a problem.

The integrated throttle control is a great feature. This lets you travel to a client's location with only the yoke and a laptop and do limited training exercises. The software will have to be initialized in the personal mode, but it beats using a joystick.

Attaching Approach Chart to Yoke: Another simple way to make the experience more realistic is to attach a yoke-mounted chart clip. Be aware that some clip types will interfere with full pitch travel. One way to work around this is to Velcro a piece of cardboard stock the size of an approach plate to the front of the yoke. The chart can then be attached to the card stock with a paper clip.

The Instructor's Station: Some desktop flight simulator software allow the use of an optional instructor's station on a separate monitor. This can be used to input real-time weather changes as well as instrument and systems failures. Unlike the setup screen where failures can be selected by the person flying, these changes can be done by the instructor on a separate monitor in a dynamic fashion without the student's knowledge.

Even if an instructor is not going to be part of the training session, a "safety pilot" can present challenges to the training pilot by inputting changes from the instructor station. The time spent will be of value to both the safety pilot and pilot, but it cannot be logged. The value to the safety pilot is that he can witness the reactions and skills of the pilot and learn from their mistakes.

If an instructor station is used, two monitors must be set up on the computer. You might need to install a dual monitor video card in your computer, if you don't already have a computer system that supports two monitors.

Trim Settings Vary Between Startups: On occasion, after restarting the simulator, you may find a nose-up trim setting even if you had a neutral trim setting on the last known shutdown. This results from a discrepancy between airspeed and power setting; use the trim wheel rather than electric trim to correct it.

Monitor Refresh Rate: Flying the simulator in "PCATD Mode" requires the monitor refresh rate to be tested. If the test fails, click "retry" and the software will adjust itself. It may take clicking retry a few times to get past the refresh test. If you continue to fail, you may need to install a new high resolution graphic card.

Simulator Session Training Items: Be sure to let your students and clients know there are required items they need to bring for each lesson on the desktop flight simulator. They should bring these items with them, regardless of whether the flight is scheduled for the aircraft or simulator. This way the student is prepared for a lesson whether it is in an aircraft or desktop flight session.

Pertinent charts, both enroute and terminal, need to be part of the required items, along with a printout of the weather for the planned route of flight. The weather printout should include enroute, terminal and forecasted conditions for the actual planned departure time. A full flight should be planned, even though this is not in an aircraft. It simply makes the simulator sessions more realistic.

You can have the student file a mock flight plan so you can go over this information when they arrive. The full flight package should be emailed to the student/client so they can visualize the plan of action before the training session. This will include your departure airport, destination airport, and time of departure, whether the flight will be conducted on airways or via direct routing. Suggest preferred routes when asking the student to plan the flight.

They should also bring their logbook, kneeboard, extra pen or pencil, pad of paper, and training manuals to review any upcoming assignments. On every training assignment they should also bring the Practical Test Standards (PTS) for the rating for which they are training, whether it is in the aircraft or simulator.

4

TRAINING METHODS

...A formal, more efficient standardized training method has been recently introduced to adapt to the demands of TAA.

FITS TRAINING CONCEPTS

Before I actually get into using a PCATD, BATD, or FTD for training, I need to discuss training methods in general. This is important, especially with the introduction of Technically Advanced Aircraft (TAA).

Until recently, pilots were trained to meet the Practical Test Standards (PTS) by instructors who taught using the maneuver-based training methods (MBT). A student was told about the maneuver, (hopefully, some ground instruction preceded the flight); the instructor demonstrated the maneuver; and then the student tried the maneuver. This show-and-then-do approach was repeated until the student reached the performance level outlined in the syllabus. Then the student would be instructed to practice the maneuver until they felt they could perform it well enough to meet the required flight test standards. The instructor would then further evaluate the student until he felt he was prepared to pass the task requirements outlined in the PTS during a FAA checkride.

The MBT has proven to be effective; indeed pilots have been trained this way since the first aircraft was produced. Recently however, requirements have changed. New complex aircraft have advanced the pilot to more of a managerial role in the cockpit. Pilots have always had to multitask, but it has been taken to a new level with the advent of the glass cockpit. A pilot not only has to be proficient with stick and rudder skills, but he also needs to perform many other complex functions to fly the newer production aircraft. Pilots also need these skills to fly older legacy production aircraft that have been upgraded with new glass panels.

The old six-pack of analog gauges is fast becoming obsolete. In fact, manufacturers are not getting new orders for aircraft that are not equipped with glass.

When you consider the introduction of the Sperry gyro horizon back in 1929, our flight training obstacles today face similar growing pains. Pioneer flight instructors had to trash the old training concepts and replace them with a new, more modern method of introducing pilots to fly on instruments.

FITS Tenets
Scenario-Based Training (SBT): A training system that uses a highly structured script of real-world experiences to address flight training objectives in an operational environment.
Single-Pilot Resource Management (SRM): The art and science of managing all the resources (both onboard the aircraft and from outside sources) available to a single pilot (prior to and during flight) to ensure that the successful outcome of the flight is never in doubt.
Learner-Centered Grading (LCG): A grading scale (an outcomes assessment) for the instructor and/or student to determine the student's level of knowledge and understanding.

What is FITS?

A formal, more efficient standardized training method has been recently introduced to adapt to the demands of TAA. It is called FAA Industry Training Standards, or FITS. In the summer of 2002, the FAA Flight Standards Division formed the FITS team to address these emerging training requirements. This team consisted of researchers from Embry-Riddle Aeronautical University, the University of North Dakota School of Aerospace and industry partners Cirrus Design, Eclipse Aviation, and Elite Air Center, a Cirrus SR22 training and fractional ownership company from Atlanta, Georgia. In addition, there was some oversight responsibility assigned to the AOPA Air Safety Foundation, GAMA, SAMA and other selected sources such as the National Association of Flight instructors. (GAMA is the General Aviation Manufacturers Association and SAMA is the Small Aircraft Manufacturers Association.)

The crux of the FITS system involves the use of realistic scenarios applied to the type of aircraft being flown. The student becomes an active participant in the progression and evaluation of her own training, and all advanced features and resources in the aircraft are used from the beginning to the end of the training syllabus.

Scenario-based training, or SBT, is not new to most professional training programs. Scientists, doctors, lawyers, astronauts, airline pilots and other highly accomplished professionals depend on this method of training to reach the excellence in technical skills required for their area of expertise. Perhaps you have been using this training prior to the official adoption by the FAA.

Personal Experience with FITS

I took the Cirrus factory training in 2003 at the University of North Dakota School of Aerospace in Duluth, Minnesota. Their program was designed around the scenario-based concept to meet the unique needs of their transitioning customers. This curriculum was proving to be a highly successful method of training new owners of the glass-equipped Cirrus aircraft. The syllabus was built around the needs for an accelerated training program that, at that time, was unique to Cirrus.

I also attended the FITS instructor training workshop at Embry-Riddle University in Daytona Beach, Florida in early 2006. I had already been using scenario-based training in my flight programs, but this was one of many seminars the FAA and the other FITS team members were conducting throughout the country. Tom Glista, the FAA FITS Program Manager, outlined the goals of the FAA and industry partners for implementing the FITS program. I encourage you to visit the official FAA website for a complete background and history of the development of FITS. You will also find detailed information about the program at http://www.faa.gov/education_research/training/fits/.

I can personally vouch for the training methods in this program. Not only is scenario-based training more effective, but it is also more fun for both instructor and student. It reduces the time required to achieve the necessary and demanding multitasking skills to fly more complex TAA. Cross-country flights are planned and executed in a way that incorporates all the operating features of every aircraft being flown.

As an instructor, you can employ scenario-based concepts to teach any new task to someone. I have been successful in using the same concepts to teach a computer skills class and other technical subjects to clients. Rather then just discussing basic pull-down menus and how to open and close documents, I start by discussing the primary features they will be able to master in this program. All the minor operating tasks they will learn can be more easily understood when each session first examines a program's function in the broadest terms.

For example, in teaching features of a GPS unit, use the GPS simulator on the ground prior to a flight. Teaching and learning the unit with SBT provides a full understanding of the operating software prior to learning the "knobology" in the aircraft. A full practice flight can be rehearsed from departure to destination with the use of the computer trainer. After several sessions of practice with the student using all features of the GPS, including autopilot, the pieces of the learning puzzle will come together rapidly. Using interactive self-evaluation reinforces learning so that both student and instructor are confident about the transfer of knowledge.

FITS Training Flexibility

FITS training standards are neither mandated by the FAA nor required for training. This makes FITS training easy to adapt for each training flight or mission profile. An instructor may realize that the FITS concept does not always apply in certain stages of training. PTS tasks need to be performed to test standards, but they can still be integrated into a mission-related lesson, such as a short flight or a desktop session to a local airport. The self-evaluation and interaction of the student is always a part of a training session, especially once the instructor understands the total FITS concept. The benefit of this is that the student feels part of the flight planning process. The end result is a logical progression of organized sessions leading to a student or client being certified or making the transition to a new aircraft or TAA.

As a flight instructor or school with a course outline and syllabus already in place, the FITS approach can be adapted to fit your program. A Part 141 flight school should consider sending their flight instructors to a flight instructor FITS training seminar. Instructors usually need to be sold on the way this training works before they can begin using it with their students.

Your insurance company may be interested in knowing you have implemented a FITS program. It might even lower your rates.

FITS APPROVED TRAINING AIDS AND PRODUCTS

Although not mandated, FITS is endorsed by the FAA and industry team members, and flight training materials, teaching aids, books and other products are now being designed to meet certain FITS-approved criteria. The PCATD, BATD, and other desktop flight simulators are also being integrated into the FITS plan.

Of all the training products, desktop simulators are one of the best tools for scenario-based training. The process begins with role playing by the instructor. For instance, if a student is starting cross-country training, the CFII can assume the role of ATC to deliver the clearance. A complete cross-country flight can be completed, which can serve as a precursor to the actual flight done in the airplane. This initial IFR session can set the stage for a relaxed and competent student during their subsequent training flight.

Assigning a Scenario-Based Lesson to a Student

Instructors and examiners often use email to send lessons or a flight test scenario to a student or applicant. This procedure works well for advanced planning of either a flight review or instrument proficiency check. This way the student/applicant can make all the preliminary decisions themselves, i.e., flight planning, weather briefing, fuel requirements and flight plan filing.

Using a desktop flight simulator, BATD, or PCATD makes for a similar means of advanced planning. The typical mission-based scenario can include the actual weather briefing for the day of the lesson, even though it might not be flown in an aircraft. The value of this format is that it advances the student's decision-making skills, allowing you to train them on risk management, situational awareness and single pilot resource management. This is especially true if the student can tackle the scenario before meeting with the instructor. You'll quickly see that a well-conceived scenario can help you teach good judgment and individual decision making, which until recently, was considered impossible to teach.

The template for any scenario begins with a certain objective and the corresponding elements for the student's stage of training. Each flight, whether simulated or real, should be challenging for the student but not exceed their abilities. A list of each lesson task to be performed is essential.

A typical scenario is not a training program unto itself. The instructor usually takes on the role of coordinator and follows up the session as an evaluator, with the student providing input of her own progress. It might begin with the basic goal of conducting an instrument approach without the aid of the acting CFII. The student then takes total responsibility for managing all the tasks involved in flying an approach without the instructor's input. They both evaluate the session afterwards. It can be difficult for the instructor to sit back and watch their student falter and not be able to help or critique. But remember, the CFII is a coach ready to assist only if required.

Scripting Scenarios

The flight lessons you present and script into a scenario for a student can be either actual missions you will accomplish in the aircraft or virtual ones you can use on the PCATD or BATD. You can rehash a recent flight that might not have gone well, or create scripts from a recent hangar session. Accident reports are an excellent source for creating a script, providing ideas for a series of "what ifs." By safely re-enacting an experience from either a personal flight or an accident report, the training pilot can suggest what action might have been taken to provide a more favorable outcome.

Your student can also take an active part in generating a script for the next scenario. This can make it more meaningful. The interaction between student and instructor as they put together the steps for a flight profile creates a greater understanding of what needs to be accomplished. I like to call this a confidence-building exercise.

A great source for a wide selection of scripted scenarios is the ASA website at www.asa2fly.com. (Search for On Top Scenarios.) You can select from ten different flight scenarios that can be downloaded for free. They are only compatible with On Top Version 9. These scripted scenarios will help you better plan for unexpected events if you practice them first on the PCATD. Believe me, they will make you sweat. They can be a little scary when you consider they were taken from real accident reports. Be sure to download and print out the readme file first. It has instructions as well as the approach charts for all ten scenarios.

These scenarios are highly challenging and interesting. You can pause and return to the beginning, or do a map freeze to find out how you are doing during any one of the exercises. Use these scenarios as a source for creating your own; you can even re-save them with modifications to fit your client and their aircraft.

Using Deductive Reasoning in FITS Training

FITS training is an excellent way to condition the process of deductive reasoning. Your students will learn to make competent and prudent decisions in a minimum amount of time. This will be especially valuable when a pilot is confronted with an emergency.

Here's an example: (This sample script will vary for the aircraft type being flown and situation encountered.)

Scenario:
Aircraft gear indicator lights do not show gear down and locked.

Pilot actions:

1. Check circuit breaker?
2. Check instrument rheostat switch set for day or night dimming.
3. If only one light is out, can another bulb be swapped to check if unlit bulb is burned out?
4. If none of the above steps solves the problem through deductive reasoning, execute emergency gear extension checklist. ***Note:*** *Don't feel rushed! This isn't a dire situation.*
5. Perform low pass near tower to have visual check of gear.
6. If gear appears down and locked to the tower, circle the area to burn off fuel as necessary.
7. At the proper time and airport, land at lowest speed possible with just enough power to keep nose wheel off runway until a gradual let down can be accomplished.
8. Just prior to the final touchdown, pop the door, shut off fuel and master switch.
9. After a complete stop, exit the aircraft in a safe manner.

This scenario along with many other anomalies can be rehearsed during a ground training session and practiced on a PCATD, BATD, or other type of simulator. The CFII can use the Instructor Station with On Top to create failures without the student knowing it. Keep in mind that using your imagination can give your practice session an extra dimension. For example, if you want to rehearse an engine failure sequence on the PCATD or BATD, you don't need the pull-type throttle on the yoke, so why not use that for carb heat. Any props or switches you can add to make the cockpit layout more realistic will help your student learn.

The Next Three Things

A primary skill in instrument flying is the ability to think ahead. I like to occasionally ask my client what they think are the next three things that will occur in this flight. With this in mind, you can develop isolated scenarios, such as setting up for an approach ten miles out, entering a hold from a random position, preparing for a procedure turn or DME arc, or practicing airway transitions.

You can create a relaxed training atmosphere that allows your student to make mistakes and be critiqued and corrected. If he bungles something entirely, it is easy to rewind, click, and drag their aircraft, or just click reset and try it again.

Learner-Centered Grading

The last essential part of the FITS teaching process is evaluation. The FITS method includes input from the student and differs from traditional grading.

The objective of scenario-based training, which is consistent with any learning process, is to change thought processes, habits, and behaviors. The FITS grading is conducted independently by the student and the CFI and then compared during the postflight critique. The student should achieve a new level of learning with each flight, so grading should be progressive.

Completion certificate from ASA G1000 interactive course.

There are two primary areas where a student is evaluated:

1. **Maneuvers/Skills/Tasks**
2. **Single-Pilot Resource Management**

Note: Both of these are judged as separate categories of learning.

They are further broken down into the following subcategories:

Maneuvers/Skills/Tasks: At the completion of the scenario, the student should fit into one of the following highest to lowest levels of learning proficiency:

Perform: Perform without assistance from CFI. *Errors and deviations will be identified and corrected by the student in an expeditious manner.* This is the highest level of learning.

Practice: Plan and execute the scenario. *Some coaching, instruction, and/or assistance from the instructor is required to correct deviations and errors.*

Explain: Be able to describe the scenario activity and understand the underlying concepts, principles, and procedures that comprise the activity. *Instructor activity is required to successfully execute the maneuver.*

Describe: Describe the physical characteristics and cognitive elements of the scenario activity. *Instructor assistance is required to successfully execute the maneuver.* This is the lowest level of learning.

Not Observed: This category is assigned to any task which is not either accomplished or required.

Single-Pilot Resource Management (SRM): At the completion of the scenario, the student should fit into one of the following highest to lowest levels of ability to conduct efficient use of SRM skills:

Manage/Decide: Can correctly gather the most important data available both within and outside the cockpit; identify possible course of action; evaluate the risk inherent in each course of action; and make the appropriate decision. Instructor intervention is not required for the safe completion of the flight.

Practice: Is able to identify, understand, and apply SRM principles to the actual flight situation. Coaching, instruction, and/or assistance from the instructor will quickly correct minor deviations and errors. The student will be an active decision maker.

Explain: Can verbally identify, describe, and understand the risks inherent in the flight scenario. The student will need to be prompted to identify risks and make decisions.

Not Observed: Any event not accomplished or required.

TRADITIONAL MANEUVERS BASED TRAINING VS. SCENARIO BASED TRAINING

A laboratory-controlled comparison of traditional maneuvers based training (MBT) and scenario based training (SBT) was conducted at Embry-Riddle Aeronautical University. The following is the results of this study as recorded by Professor Jon French (used by permission):

A laboratory-controlled comparison of traditional maneuvers based training (MBT) and scenario based training (SBT) is described during the acquisition of technically advanced aircraft (TAA) instrument flight skills in a flight training device (FTD). All 27 participants were instrument-rated pilots with less than 500 total flight hours and virtually no experience with TAA. All were randomly assigned to the MBT or SBT condition. All received eight hours of MBT or SBT before the final post-test evaluation. The TAA FTD was a Cirrus SR20 with a Chelton primary flight display (PFD) and multi-function display (MFD) powered by Microsoft Flight Simulator (2002). Experimentally blind expert raters scored instrument flight skills during a pre-training (pre-test) and a similar post-training (post-test) data collection flights. Pre- and post-tests were scored for eight phases of flight (e.g. Take off, Approach, Missed Approach).

Subjective attitude, workload (NASA TLX) and situational awareness questionnaires were completed after both flights. On most of the measures, significant improvement was found between pre-test and post-test scores, indicating that both MBT and SBT are effective. In addition, the SBT Group performed statistically better on five of the eight measures of piloting ability (three of the five, Autopilot use, Approach and Missed Approach phases of flight, are shown below) than the MBT for the post-test flight, using a Mann Whitney U distribution free comparison. In no case did the SBT Group score worse than the MBT group. Further, the SBT Group demonstrated a tendency to report reduced workload (NASA TLX graph below) and an improvement in self-efficacy and situational awareness compared to the MBT. The results indicate that SBT may lead to improved piloting and navigation skills over traditional maneuvers based training for TAA flight. Although MBT is a reliable method to teach instrument flight and has been used for decades, SBT, which is recommended by the FAA Industry Training Standards (FITS) program, may be a better strategy for TAA instrument flight skill acquisition.

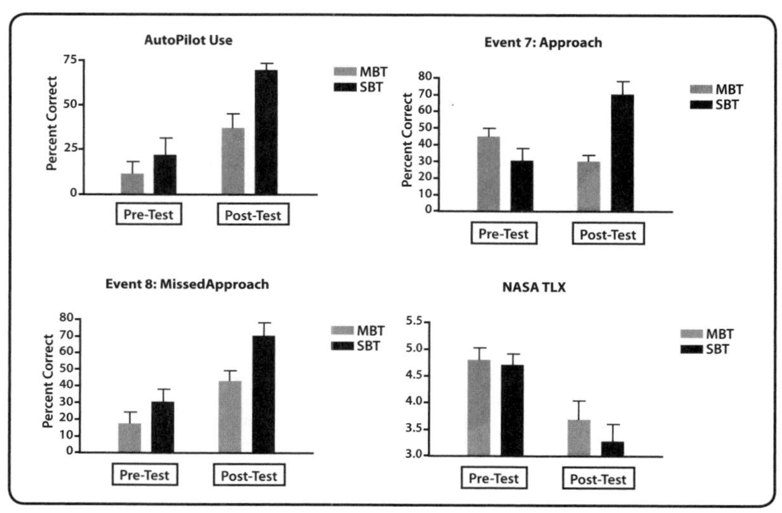

Results of the Embry-Riddle study.

5

GETTING STARTED

...If you don't properly set the scene, your first demonstration of the simulator will be followed by a session of over - controlling inputs by the student.

THE FIRST DESKTOP FLIGHT SIMULATOR SESSION

The first session with your student on the PCATD or BATD will set the tone for the rest of your training. If you are not sold on the value and usefulness of the simulator, your student will know immediately. You need to be enthusiastic and professional in your approach and have total knowledge of all operational features. This will require you to spend your own time mastering the feel and operation of the simulator.

Before you begin the session, have the simulator loaded with your student's personal aircraft instrument panel. Preload the local airport position and line the aircraft up on the active runway. This helps to eliminate delays in setup time. In future sessions, explain how the student can set the startup parameters themselves.

Have the student sit down and get comfortable in front of the machine. Talk them through the whole instrument panel and explain the desktop simulator control features. This might take about 15–20 minutes.

This next step will surprise you. Do not let the student "fly" the PCATD until you first sit down and demonstrate taking off and flying to an altitude with the student watching your control inputs and technique. This will give them the knowledge they need to control the PCATD to your expectations. After level off, pause the apparatus and let them sit down and get comfortable again.

Before you take it out of pause mode, explain that the desktop simulator will not fly like an aircraft and that it is primarily a teaching tool to develop scanning skills and procedures. Explain that any desktop flight simulator will be harder to control than the aircraft and is very *pitch* sensitive. Explain that the PCATD will often amplify the errors one might make in the aircraft, such as over controlling and scanning poorly.

Next, remind the student where the pause mode button is located and have them push it when they feel they are ready to become a "virtual" pilot. This initial sequence of setting the scene is crucial. If not followed as described, the first training session will be frustrating, and the student will tend to over-control inputs in the next session. This is the nature of any desktop flight simulator.

After some straight and level practice, evaluate whether the student can hold altitude and heading within reasonable limits, say plus or minus 200 feet/10 degrees. If this is a problem after 10–15 minutes of observation, pause the PCATD and review scanning techniques.

Follow a Syllabus

It is important to follow an approved syllabus from the very first lesson, especially if this is to be a logged PCATD session. For some examples, see Appendix A in this book for a Private Pilot BATD syllabus, and Appendix B for an Instrument Rating PCATD syllabus.

Using the syllabus, brief the student on what the first simulator lesson will entail. This allows them to ask about scanning methods or other questions they might have. This would be a good time to bring up the control and performance concept, or the idea of primary/supporting instruments. The session should also cover the primary flight instruments, the pitot/static system, fuel management and configuring the PCATD.

After getting used to the characteristics of the PCATD with some basic straight and level flight, ask the student to push the pause button. You might introduce the autopilot early in the training to show how it can keep the aircraft on heading. Then have them tune a VOR or copy a simple clearance. Using altitude hold is also a good way to get the airplane trimmed if you find the student performing poorly because of inexperience with the trim. This falls in line with conventional FITS methods: Make use of all available resources during training and build early habits that emphasize SRM.

Integration, especially on a first session, should be accomplished with ground, PCATD and flight time in the aircraft. This helps reinforce the transfer of knowledge that will reveal understanding early in the training.

PCATD / LESSON 3

Objective:

For the student to gain understanding of the straight climb and descent, and turns, during instrument flight.

Content:

- ❑ The straight climb
  - ❑ Climbing at different airspeeds
  - ❑ Variations on entering the climb
  - ❑ Climbing at a particular rate
- ❑ The straight descent
  - ❑ Climbing away from a descent
  - ❑ Descending at a particular rate
  - ❑ The precision approach
- ❑ Turning
  - ❑ Bank angle and rate of turn
  - ❑ Roll-in and roll-out rate
  - ❑ The medium level turn
  - ❑ Instrument turns to a specific heading
  - ❑ Climbing turns
  - ❑ Descending turns
  - ❑ Steep level turn
  - ❑ Steep climbing turn
  - ❑ Steep descending turn
- ❑ Pattern A
- ❑ Pattern H
- ❑ Review ground tracks

Assignment:

Instrument Flying, Chapters 5 and 6

Completion Standards:

The student must successfully complete all review questions following the assigned reading, and effectively control the airplane within 200 feet, 20 degrees, and 20 knots, keeping all turns coordinated.

Sample lesson from PCATD syllabus; see Appendix B for the complete "Instrument Rating PCATD syllabus".

Develop Workload Management Skills in the First Lesson

The PCATD is an excellent tool for developing workload management skills. Emphasize and develop that with students, beginning with the first lesson. Start with multitasking exercises that begin with a few dispersed items, such as setting the altimeter, setting a VOR frequency, or opening a chart. Explain that scanning is always the pilot's primary focus. Keeping the needles where they belong only requires a brief glance away from the primary gauges, sometimes referred to as a "peek." A secondary task can then be accomplished before the student needs to return to the basic six to be sure all is well. It might take two or more peeks to complete the secondary task (such as folding a chart), but it is the only way to keep the aircraft where it belongs when hand flying.

The student must learn to prioritize tasks. Keeping the virtual cockpit organized, setting radio frequencies, writing down expected altitudes and clearances are just a few of the tasks that need to be done when time permits. It is never too early to begin working on these skills; they are compulsory in the aircraft. The simulator environment is a great place to start building good habits.

Introduce IFR Required Instrument Checks

Sitting in front of a flight simulator provides a great way to discuss and perform the instrument check items required for IFR flight. The 24-month altimeter/pitot-static system and transponder check can be covered, along with the 30-day VOR checks. Even the different methods for doing VOR checks can be performed on a PCATD.

Set Limits

Any desktop simulator is a great place to develop discipline in your instrument scan. You should teach your student he should not be satisfied until all the individual instruments are consistently held where they belong. It all starts with heading and altitude. Teach them that everything else will fall into place, including a predetermined course that will keep the navigation instruments within quarter scale.

Desktop simulators are more pitch sensitive than aircraft; therefore, holding altitude demands gentle pitch control and immediate action when the VSI begins to show a climb or descent. If proper scanning and control inputs keep this under control, holding altitude to within 50 feet should be feasible. It's important to note the simulator's VSI lag is programmed to match that of an airplane, but the action of the needle, once it starts moving, is exaggerated.

Heading control can be more easily maintained if the heading indicator is kept primary for wings level. Just like in an aircraft, if his scan doesn't fixate on one instrument too long, and proper interpretation is maintained, your student can easily keep tight limits on heading within five degrees.

Even after getting everything properly set up and trimmed, it is difficult to have a simulator fly totally hands off for more than just a few minutes. However, this design trait is not a bad feature. It just means your student needs to understand how a better scan will keep their skills sharp. Instrument students have said they were glad to get back in the air because the aircraft trims and flies better. Usually a longer transgression from the instruments can be made without drifting off heading or altitude in the aircraft. Noticing this, they understand that the flight simulator is making them a better pilot.

Screen shot of scenario setup.

Save the Flight Scenarios

Most desktop flight simulators include a feature that allows the user to save a scenario for a future session. This is a valuable way to track progress. Do this from the first lesson, including saving startup parameters. As basic as the first lesson might be, this habit will save time and increases the usefulness of the simulator.

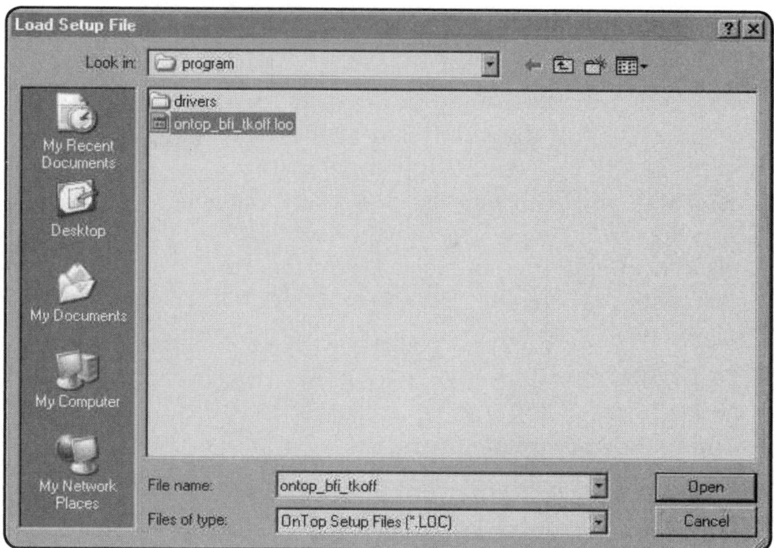

Don't Push the Envelope

You can't expect perfect performance when first sitting behind the PCATD flight controls. If after several lessons or sessions, you need to input more challenging flight characteristics, enter turbulence and heavier winds into the setup. Whatever the actual aircraft skill level of your student, you need to understand and communicate the value of the simulator. It is a training tool, and the student should not expect it to handle like an aircraft.

Keep Your Cool

One of the worst things that can happen when working with a student is to lose your cool. In some instances this can lead to a verbal showdown. The first couple of hours establishes a bond between you and student. If it is obvious that friction exists at this point, have the student work with someone else. It is best to be honest and tell the student you feel there is a personality conflict. Another instructor might work out just fine, and there is no shame in recognizing this. It is a fact of life; not everyone is compatible. Try to keep your personal biases and differences out of the picture. It helps ensure your student gets a fair evaluation.

Accepting the Appropriate Dress

Wardrobe can be a hot topic when it comes to what is appropriate for professional flight instructors. Most national flight schools require instructors to dress with a white shirt and tie. How you dress makes an initial impression about you as a professional. Once you establish a respectful relationship with your student, a more relaxed attire will be appropriate. It doesn't make sense to wear a tie or suit coat in a climate where the temperatures and humidity are unbearably high. Even in today's highly structured corporate world, most executives dress more casually.

After the first day of training, the knowledge and respect you portray will override any informal attire. Generally, it is appropriate to match your student's style of dress, to a reasonable degree. However, anything less than clean business casual would be truly inappropriate.

Some Pilots Aren't Going to Adapt

It is rare, but there is a possibility you may encounter someone who is a great instrument pilot in the airplane, but who is totally turned off by computer simulators. They either want to fly a real airplane or just dislike simulators in general. They may not be open to change, so give them the benefit of the doubt and do all the training in their aircraft. Perhaps they want to build more hours in the air and don't have the patience to learn to use and practice on a computer replica. Do not argue with them, but respect their wishes. You are in fact working for them.

Selecting an Examiner

You should feel confident that your student or applicant will pass the flight check with any designated pilot examiner (DPE) of his choice. The preparation work you have done should assure confidence in you and your student that they will pass the first time.

It helps to have a preliminary chat with any new examiner you might be using. This is not necessarily to get an overview of what will be asked on the oral, or the flight maneuvers that will be performed. The idea here is to establish a rapport with the examiner. Try to have the student meet them prior to the actual checkride. This is very important to help break the ice.

You should not totally rely on a single DPE for all your checkrides. There will be a certain quota of first-time busts they are expected to meet. If you keep feeding a single examiner all your students, you might eventually get on the hit list. It also says a lot about your teaching ability if you can send applicants to several examiners and still have an 85–90% first time pass rate.

The best preparation you can do for your student, the examiner and yourself, is to properly fill out the 8710 application form. Most examiners accept a neatly completed application in black ink or filled out on the Internet. Keep a copy for yourself. The examiners I use like to have an applicant note in the aircraft logbooks when the annual or 100-hour inspections were performed. I refer to these notes for required maintenance on the ELT battery, altimeter, static system and transponder. Beginning March 1, 2007, all examiners and CFIs are being asked to use the IACRA (Integrated Airman Certification and/or Rating Application) online system to fill out the 8710 application form.

Have your student use a checklist to remember the required items for the day of the checkride. That way they are less likely to forget something. This list can include items you want to brief your student on, as you wouldn't want him to have to go back to the examiner because of something you forgot.

Instructor's Role and Responsibility

The instructor's main goal is to transfer his knowledge to the student and evaluate how well the student can safely perform the tasks required to obtain the rating or level of proficiency at hand. A fine line exists between knowing when to take over the controls and when to let consequences do the instructing. A basic student pilot requires more demonstration by the instructor, while the instrument student rarely needs the instructor to take over the controls of the aircraft.

I find that my need to fly the aircraft as an instrument instructor is usually limited to the unusual attitude setup during instrument flight training. This is the only time I feel that I should take the controls, unless a safety situation arises that calls for intervention. In many instances, a student will strongly object to the instructor doing too much flying; after all, they are paying for the flight experience. On the other hand, the CFII is the acting pilot-in-command and responsible for the outcome of every flight.

As mentioned before, it is common for the beginning instrument student to over control the aircraft. They might comment, "It seems like there is a lot of turbulence today." This can usually be resolved by focusing on trim. Have them trim the aircraft and then release the controls. Even on a fairly turbulent day, the plane will be quite stable. Odds are they were using more control input than what was needed.

It takes a lot of patience to sit back and let someone make mistakes. Many instrument students are going to overdo their basic aircraft control, and it is not going to disappear within a few hours. Ten hours of solid instrument training goes a long way toward improving control issues. Students must spend enough time practicing the basics, or it will come back to haunt them (and you) when it comes time for instrument approaches. An instrument student needs to know early on that they can usually perform well flying IFR, if they can control altitude and heading precisely.

I find the best technique for teaching ILS approaches is to let the student fly the first few approaches without using foggles. They soon realize just how small a heading and descent change is needed to keep the needles trapped in the doughnut. This technique is not practiced by many instructors, so I've seen students fight the porpoising effect longer then they would otherwise.

Your instrument students should do all the radio work. It is tempting to jump in and speak to the controllers when things get busy, but let your students handle the transmissions. This is the only way they can learn the jargon and work through the fear of talking on the radio. Your role is basically to advise if things get out of hand.

Checkride Sign-off

Sometimes students will pressure you for a checkride endorsement. You are not doing the student or yourself any favors by giving a premature sign-off if you are not confident they can pass.

To take the pressure off, give the student a practice checkride with an honest performance evaluation. This should include both the oral and practical requirements, as set forth in the Practical Test Standards. The parameters are clearly stated in the PTS and if the student cannot reasonably meet these, he is not ready for the real checkride. I don't expect a perfect performance to these standards, but I do require a minimum 75–80% level of proficiency. You won't get much argument from students who have failed to perform to FAA standards. They realize they need more work and dedicated preparation.

The ten-day training program I often teach gives students a limited window within which to get instrument trained, but I never contend that everyone can be ready in ten days. The practice checkride is rehearsed on day nine with a clear understanding that if standards are not met, the student will need to spend more time preparing. It is possible some students may not be ready for a practice or mock checkride on the ninth day.

Taking a Practice Checkride on a Desktop Flight Simulator

Let's say the weather doesn't cooperate on the day of your intended practice checkride with your student. He is ready and charged up for the big day, but the weather is below minimums. Does this mean you have to wait to give a fair evaluation of his performance in an aircraft before you can sign off the 8710? The answer is absolutely not, as long as your student has met all the required flight hours in the aircraft.

If you feel your student has been performing on a consistent level for all the required flight tasks in the aircraft, there should be nothing to keep you from doing a final evaluation on a desktop flight simulator. In fact, holding someone back due to weather conditions on the day of the practice checkride could unnecessarily delay an actual checkride that might be scheduled for the following day. This is especially true if you feel the student is ripe to take the ride, but only needs some brushing up to knock off the rough edges.

6

FLIGHT VISUALIZATION

...Armchair flying has been around for years and the old timers know it is what makes their flights routine.

FLYING WITHOUT WINGS

Some of the best practice flying an instrument pilot can do is with visualization techniques, which can be employed without the need for an aircraft or simulator. If your student hasn't been doing this as a pilot, she has been missing some quality "virtual" flight experiences. Armchair flying has been around for years, and old-timers know it's what makes their flights routine. There are several ways you can teach practice flying.

You may have seen a charter or ferry pilot looking into space as he sipped his coffee in the lounge of your local airport. He might have been reflecting on the night before, but chances are, he was rehearsing for the next leg of his flight. It all happens up in the gray matter, and it pays big dividends once airborne.

It is wise to have your student armchair fly the complete flight before launching. Ask them to think about the following: Is this flight to a familiar airport? Do they expect to encounter some challenging weather? Is the routing familiar? All these factors are good reasons to rehearse a flight. To get started, have your student gather the charts and flight plans she'll be using. The process of mentally flying her trip will help your student ensure she is organized. It will help her remember the important details, such as fuel stops, load factors and having the airplane staged on the ramp.

Armchair Flight

To mentally step through an upcoming flight, have your client or student trace the sequence of actions as they are likely to unfold, which typically begins with the flight plan. Filling out the flight plan provides a mental picture of what is to be accomplished.

Next, have your student lay out the enroute and approach charts, which will get their mind prepared for the total scope of the flight. Instructors often refer to "finger flying" the route and approach as a systematic way of thinking through the flight or approach to landing. This is a particularly useful tool to prepare for the unexpected—the missed approach. Executing the missed approach will be a much simpler task if the student has visualized the conditions. The "finger-flying" exercise helps them fully understand if there are any unusual procedures to follow.

Many desktop flight simulators have "conditionals" built into the setup options. This typically includes the ability to vary the weather by a plus/minus factor, or fail an instrument or system. Be sure to use these variables when setting up a flight for your student, as they let you see how he will respond to an unexpected event. Did he select the alternate when the current route was getting below minimums? Did he execute the missed approach when the runway environment was lost? Did she recognize the failed instrument or system and cover it up or otherwise begin a cross-check against the other instruments? These "what-if" scenarios, performed in the safety and comfort of the desktop flight simulator, are very beneficial to the student. Pause the system, talk about the situation, back it up for another shot under varying conditions. These tools make the visualization process a truly valuable experience prior to the actual flight.

A PCATD or similar device is the ultimate aid when it comes to visualizing a practice flight. It adds an extra element of realism to the rehearsal process, but is not a necessity. Remember, the human mind can be one of the best simulators you will ever use.

Tips for a Valuable Experience

Realistic brain training can start with personal past experience, when things didn't go quite right, or stories you have read in magazines. If you need more scenarios, check the NTSB website for a history of past accident files. This provides a background of the good, bad and ugly. These scenarios can be "re-flown" by thinking through the error chain that may have led to a minor mishap or serious accident. Often it is the links of the accident chain that compound a pilot's mistakes and lead to disaster.

Encourage your clients or students to brain fly with their pilot friends. They can exchange opinions and suggestions on what might have happened. Many pilots refer to this as hangar flying. Some of these sessions can get quite lively and be a source for some of the most valuable lessons learned in piloting.

Encourage your students to use of all their senses in the planning exercises. They should think about the sights, sounds, feelings and smells experienced in the aircraft. An electrical fire produces a particular odor that is different than smoke from exhaust fumes. An impending stall has a unique and uneasy feeling on the flight controls. The sight picture of a normal landing has a typical view out the windscreen. All of these can be hashed out in hangar flying or during brain flying sessions with a friend.

For example, an engine in a particular aircraft has a known and familiar sound on take off, cruise, approach and landing. Start your hangar flying session with this knowledge and ask what you would do if the sound changes. Then apply deductive reasoning to evaluate and improve the situation.

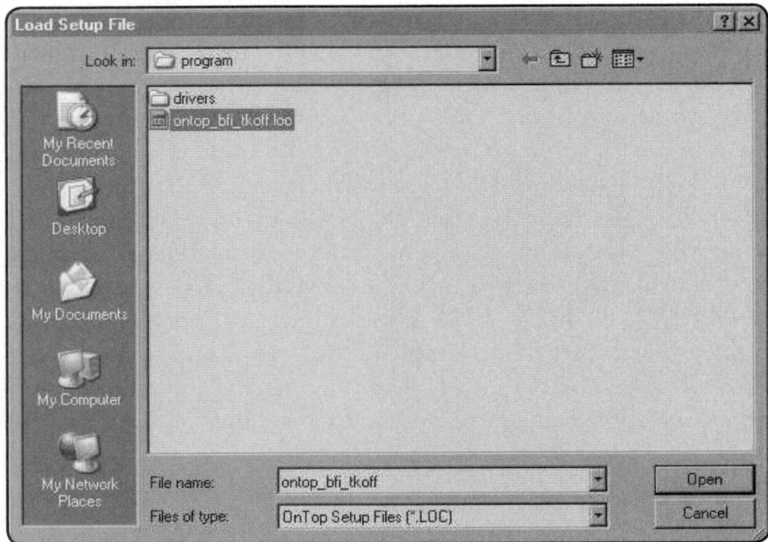

Use the On Top "Setup" functions to brain train by building scenarios from the experience of others, hangar stories, or NTSB reports.

Using Armchair Flying for Flight Test Preparation

An applicant can review the practical test standards and the Pilot's Operating Handbook (POH) as they brain fly through a complete checkride. Encourage your students to make this part of their preparations a day or two before they are scheduled for a checkride.

If an applicant is having a difficult time mastering a task for the checkride, try to break down each maneuver step-by-step. What might seem like an overwhelmingly complex task can be less intimidating if done through the gray matter of the brain cells. Visualization is a great way to build confidence prior to a checkride.

Self-Evaluation through Brain Flight

Mentally reviewing a flight after completion can be one of the most beneficial means of self-evaluation. How well did you hold altitude and heading during the enroute and approach phases of flight? Did you make any errors reading back clearances? Were all the navigation instruments within quarter scale during the flight? Review and analyze the details, as this exercise will provide a productive evaluation.

Humor in the Cockpit

One of the best defenses against stress is to not take life too seriously. It is one of your best techniques for loosening up your student prior to a checkride or when you see their performance regressing. I am not one to have a lot of jokes on the tip of my tongue or deliver them nonstop. Fortunately this is not required to create humor in the cockpit. Often, conversation on the radio is a real belly-buster, and if you and your student are part of it, that's fine.

One time I was performing holding practice with a student over a VOR near a controlled airport. We had to monitor the tower for advisories as we flew the holds. A pilot reported he was inbound, had the ATIS and would report on final for the active runway. The tower, not to be second guessed, came back with instructions not to enter on final, but proceed and report on downwind. The pilot quipped, "pilot nothing, controller one."

After landing, the pilot was instructed to contact ground control when clear of the runway. He forgot to change frequencies and called the tower for taxi instructions. While monitoring the frequency, I could not resist the temptation to say, "pilot nothing, controller two." The pilot meekly said, "You've got that right."

My student, who was struggling with holding entries, was as humored by this as the tower. His tension lessened and his performance improved. This is just one example of the many funny things that can happen while flying.

Another time one of my students was completing his runup. He had checked the mags and exercised the prop. The flight controls were next. With a quizzical look, he watched out my window at the aileron, and pulled the yoke back and forth.

I couldn't believe it when he said the controls were not operating properly and continued to move the yoke in the fore and aft direction while watching the right aileron stay neutral!

Errors like this are not serious. They are simply momentary lapses in reason that happen to overworked students, even the best ones. If anything, it provides an opportunity to laugh and realize we are all human. It dramatizes how instrument flying requires concentrated thought, so that small "brain fades" don't turn into serious incidents.

If in Doubt, Confirm

Students should be taught to advocate their position if a dispute arises with controllers. To politely argue for themselves if they feel they are right is healthy and appropriate, and how to do this should be part of their training.

How many times have you been instructing a student, when the controller issues a heading or altitude assignment that you and your student hear differently? If you have been teaching for a few years, you know this can happen.

If the student automatically assumes you are correct because you are the instructor, that is the wrong assumption. Students should be taught to query the controller and verify assigned headings and altitudes. This is the proper way to handle the situation whether or not an instructor is on board. It might be embarrassing to find that you were wrong, but it teaches students to always confirm instructions.

The same philosophy should be applied anytime ATC issues a potentially hazardous instruction. For example, if you were given an altitude assignment that could put your aircraft into icing conditions, it should be challenged. Another situation might involve an extended flight over water in a single-engine aircraft without life jackets, etc., on board. Or, consider the case where a heading assignment would penetrate a thunderstorm.

Your best response to ATC, when asked to do something that could jeopardize the flight, is "UNABLE." You do not even have to respond with an immediate explanation. The main point is to get the controller's attention and communicate your situation right away. A single word with the aircraft ID transmission is often the most effective way to do this. A quality instructional program should teach students that this is a key part of the pilot's role.

TRAITS OF A GOOD INSTRUMENT PILOT

Through the years of training students, I have found some common traits that make good instrument pilots. Students may not display these talents initially, but they can develop them with further training. All traits are equally important, so they are not listed in any order of priority.

Multitasker. Pilots must be able to juggle several tasks at once while keeping the aircraft on course and at altitude. If a student gets too focused on a power setting while the airplane wanders off, you need to work with them on developing theirs skills related to multitasking.

Self-disciplined. A student with the discipline to work continuously at staying on altitude and heading is well on their way to being a good instrument pilot. Basically, this is what keeps the plane where it belongs en route or during the approach phase of flying on an IFR flight plan.

Good judgment. This is one trait that's hard to teach. Still, instrument pilots must know the limits of their aircraft and have safe personal weather minimums. When the decision is made to stay on the ground, it must be a firm one. An instrument instructor must be able to evaluate a student's ability to make good decisions.

Tenacious. Instrument students and pilots need to be tenacious. I have trained some pilots who started off not doing very well, but once they began training, they never gave up and went on to become very competent instrument pilots. This characteristic is also important in flight for those times when pilots have to cope with adversity. A word of caution: This is an area that needs to be tempered with good judgment. Being overly zealous or results-oriented can lead to dangerous behavior, such as duck-under syndrome.

Good response time. Instrument pilots need to act decisively and with good response time. Those who are slow to move or lag behind will take longer to train. A student may begin a move toward a pre-landing item, then retreat. This is usually due to a lack of experience—they don't know what sequence is correct. But in general, tentativeness is not a good trait for pilots.

Being organized. People who are naturally organized possess an important skill for instrument flying. There is nothing more useful for single pilot IFR than having all the needed charts organized and handy. Inevitably, a dropped pencil or chart will end up directly under your seat and require you to move your seat back to get it. This experience does wonders for your trim and temper control! Ask any experienced instrument pilot; Murphy's Law can happen to the most organized person.

Good communication. Lastly, good communication is vital. The ability to say what you want in the least number of words using proper terminology will get you favors from ATC. Controllers will acknowledge professional transmissions and help make your flight smoother.

Don't be disappointed if your students lack these personality traits early on. Again, they can be acquired with experience. Being able to pinpoint your students' weaknesses will help you better tailor their instruction.

TRANSITIONING TO INSTRUMENTS

… But somehow you start to believe the clouds are providing a true reference for wings level and you start distrusting what you learned in basic instrument training—to always trust your instruments.

RECOGNIZING GYRO SYSTEM FAILURES AND HOW TO DEAL WITH THEM

In some ways, it was almost easier to recognize and deal with a panel failure before full glass cockpit aircraft came along. Certainly they're more reliable, but it can be quite another story when dealing with the failure, especially in actual IMC.

The partial panel skills everyone learns in basic instrument training are essential; the primary objective is to maintain control of the aircraft by using backup flight instruments. With glass equipment, the pilot needs to interpret a different display configuration to maintain control of the aircraft, but the principles are the same: cross-check to identify the failure and then use the other instruments.

A number of aircraft accidents can be attributed to failure of the primary gyro source of power, or an instrument failure that confuses the pilot. Even the best-trained and competent pilot can be misled by conflicting information from the attitude and heading indicators. Neither of these instruments on a traditional vacuum source aircraft will cause immediate and total failure. They just seem to die a slow death. However, there is a moment of doubt for most pilots about which instrument is wrong, particularly flying in IMC.

Learning to recognize a failed instrument or system is one of the most important skills you can teach your students. The desktop flight simulator is the ideal tool for this lesson because of the ability to pause and discuss, back up to change the circumstances, or refly under different conditions.

Setup for Distrust

Rapid head movement in IMC can temporarily cause the pilot to distrust what the primary flight instruments are indicating. This can happen when lowering your head to pick up a chart or turning in the cockpit to talk to a passenger.

One of the most disconcerting things that can cause false illusions about which end is up in the aircraft happens at night when flying above a perfectly flat undercast layer. The stars are bright and the moon is full, but you don't believe the instrument indications, which are showing a slight turn. Your wings appear level based on your reference to the cloud deck, but somehow you start to believe the clouds are providing a true reference for wings level. So you start distrusting what you learned in basic instrument training—to always trust your instruments. If this hasn't happened to you in your flying experience, let me be the first to tell you it can scramble the best instrument pilots as they begin drifting off course and have yet to realize what is happening.

The best way to approach flying in IMC is to trust that the aircraft instruments are presenting the true attitude, especially when total reference to the natural horizon is not an option. Flying in and out of cloud layers during an approach can present one of the most hazardous conditions for instrument distrust. Glass paneled aircraft with PFD and MFDs, however, make staying focused on the instruments a lot less challenging.

They don't always tell the truth—cross-check.

Partial Panel Flying

The hardest part of flying partial panel is deciding which instrument has failed in the first place. Unfortunately, during instructional flights, it doesn't cut it for the CFI to cover up instruments because doing this doesn't do justice to the real nature of instrument failure. Nor does it reproduce the confusion that occurs. Essentially, it comes down to the instrument cross-check, which compares each of the primary flight instrument indications and initiates a majority rules process of elimination. The inverted V-scan is considered the most effective cross-check for troubleshooting failure because it samples information from each source of instrument power—vacuum, electrical and pitot/static.

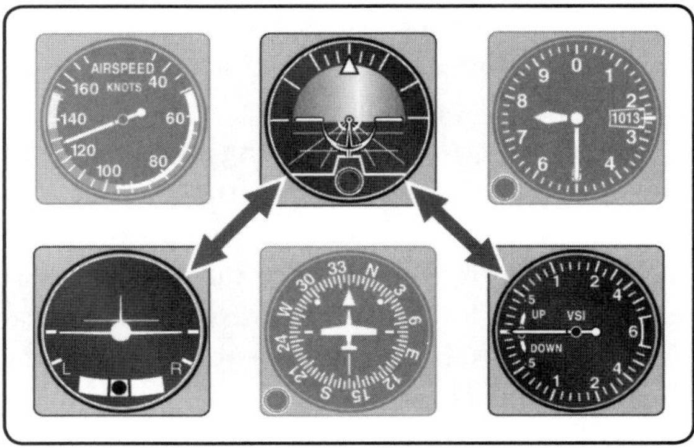

Inverted V-scan.

A warning flag or failure light is a good first indication of which instrument or system failed. Next, check the suction gauge if you are flying a traditional vacuum-powered primary driven instrument paneled aircraft. If it is a glass paneled aircraft, check the individual power source indicators to determine if all available components are providing output.

It might surprise you to know that most instrument-rated and current pilots are not partial panel proficient. This is especially true in complex aircraft when some pilots could enter a deadly spiral before recognizing a complete instrument failure. In an airplane with traditional instruments, there is no way to accurately simulate a source failure such as loss of a vacuum pump. Therefore, the only way to do this training realistically is with a desktop flight simulator. In On Top, a programmed vacuum failure will cause those instruments to slowly lose accuracy as the gyros spool down. This is an excellent way to give your students a sense of the resulting confusion. The software has a soap-dish cover feature that allows you to cover up an instrument by clicking on it. Once the student has identified the failure and taken corrective action, they can begin practicing partial panel.

Whether you are flying a glass cockpit, a traditional equipped aircraft or a PCATD, remember to make small control inputs and keep your turns standard rate. Head for VMC if possible, and call ATC to tell them of your situation. No doubt about it, they will put you at the top of the priority list.

Remember, the majority of the 207,000 airplanes in the general aviation fleet have vacuum-powered attitude indicators and heading indicators. Many of those same airplanes are not equipped with backup or secondary attitude indicators, or a backup vacuum pump. The following study proves that even the best instrument pilot can have extreme difficulty in flying partial panel in other than the most ideal conditions.

Partial Panel Practice in the PCATD

The FAA conducted a comprehensive study in October 2002 during which 41 instrument-rated pilots were exposed to an unannounced failure of attitude and heading instrumentation during flight in single-engine general aviation aircraft: 25 in a Piper Archer PA-28 and 16 in a Beechcraft Bonanza A36.

The PA-28 flights consisted of three groups:

- Group A was exposed to a failure of the attitude indicator (AI) and directional gyro (DG).
- Group B was exposed to the same as Group A but received 30 minutes of partial-panel instruction in a personal computer-based aviation training device (PCATD) prior to the flight.
- Group C was exposed to the same as Group A but had a failure-annunciator light (vacuum) on the panel.

The A36 flights consisted of two groups:

- Group A was exposed to a failure of the AI only.
- Group B was exposed to a failure of the AI and the horizontal situation indicator (HSI).

All the PA-28 pilots maintained control of the aircraft; 68 percent flew successful partial-panel approaches and likely would have survived if it had been an actual emergency. However, 25 percent of the Bonanza pilots could not maintain control, and the evaluator had to assume control of the aircraft. *Use of the PCATD prior to the data flight reduced the time required to recognize a failure while airborne* (mean A&C = 7.6 min., mean for B = 4.9 min.), but there were no other observed differences in performance between the Archer groups. Based on study results, the FAA made recommendations for both training and instrumentation.

Research aircraft with modified windows and goggles.

It is interesting to note that this study was conducted in an aircraft fitted with a modified polarized orange-amber material on the interior windows. This effectively blinded the volunteer pilot to the outside world. Polarized material was placed across the lower portion of the windscreen and left side window of each aircraft so that approximately the lower two-fifths of the windscreen was covered. The Francis hood used to simulate IMC contained the same polarized material in the eye openings, oriented 90° to the windshield material. This arrangement allowed the pilots to see inside the cockpit, but eliminated the outside view immediately above the glare shield.

In reference to Chapter 1, where I discuss the history of view-limiting devices, this type of modification might be considered for future instrument training to more realistically block the outside view of a training pilot.

TRUSTING THE GLASS COCKPIT

The FAA has classified TAA as aircraft that have a minimum of an IFR-certified GPS navigation system with a moving map display and an integrated autopilot. Some TAA also have a multifunction display (MFD) that shows weather, traffic and terrain graphics. In general, TAA are aircraft in which the pilot interfaces with one or more computers in order to aviate, navigate or communicate.

There is no doubt that the glass cockpit is here to stay. And although there is no FAA mandate that a pilot must take specialized training to fly an advanced TAA panel, anyone flying in serious weather would be acutely incapable of doing so without appropriate training. When the glass cockpit airliners first entered service, most GA pilots never envisioned glass displays in smaller aircraft. Obviously that thinking is behind us.

Flight Instructor Challenges

Most flight instructors are honest enough to admit they lack the necessary experience to take on a student in a glass cockpit aircraft, if they themselves are not totally knowledgeable about the equipment. Common sense dictates that a CFI would become familiar with any new avionics in an aircraft used for instruction.

Unfortunately, if you call ahead to most aircraft rental fleets to get checked out in a new glass paneled Cessna, you might be surprised to find no formalized transition training is required. It can even be tough to get training material at the FBO. Usually, the renter must buy the cockpit reference guide on their own and study prior to renting the aircraft. Past experience has shown that in come cases, the

Typical analog instrument panel.

A Garmin G1000 glass panel.

renter might even have more knowledge about the glass panel than the instructor doing the checkout.

This will change as the CFI community gets up to speed with TAA aircraft. The fact that the new glass panel avionics have deeply hidden features is not a secret. This is one reason the pilot must know how to access information quickly with minimum head-down time. A pilot who is not proficient with the avionics can be a danger when flying one of these high tech machines. It takes a few hours behind a glass panel to gain confidence in the scan, and many pilots feel the biggest obstacle to transitioning is in interpreting tape displays.

It Doesn't End with the Panel

Not only must you learn how to interpret and use the new instruments, but you also need to know what drives them. Prior to glass paneled aircraft, the vacuum and electrical power system was simple. There were fewer circuit breakers or fuses, and the schematics could fit on one page in the Pilot's Operating Handbook.

Troubleshooting problems in new aircraft requires greater knowledge. This isn't to say that we have entered such a complex environment that it overloads the single pilot. It just means more background knowledge is required for the pilot to become comfortable and competent in these aircraft.

Fortunately, training can be done with self-taught computer interactive programs. The Internet can also be used to access most of the glass panel avionics handbooks. However, nothing beats the one-on-one instruction that a competent and knowledgeable CFI or factory representative can provide.

One main consideration when transitioning to glass equipped aircraft is that they are totally reliant on electrical power for both primary and backup instrumentation. This means that a new pilot checking out in an aircraft with a PFD and/or MFD must be completely familiar with how the electrical system works. They must know how to eliminate any nonessential avionics or instruments when an emergency electrical failure occurs. They need to know where the circuit breaker panel is and how to use it without too much head-down time.

Instructor Liability

I sleep well at night without worries of students suing me. My reason is simple: I do the best job I can to ensure quality instruction and keep good records to prove it.

Student logbooks do not provide enough space to show all the training needed to meet regulations or, worse yet, prove in a court of law that you provided all that was necessary. Logbooks were designed back in the days when people did not sue at the drop of a hat. Besides, the student takes these basic training records with them, so you would have nothing to show that you completed the necessary training if you totally relied on their logs for record-keeping.

I keep a more detailed description of the training in a separate document and have the student sign this after each training segment. If doing primary instruction, you obviously have a higher chance of being sued since you are not in the aircraft to control all possible events.

If you would sleep better at night knowing you have some type of instructor liability insurance, by all means, purchase it. But you should still maintain adequate records to protect yourself.

MENTOR ARTICLE BY THE AUTHOR
(permission granted for reprint from NAFI)

I'm from the old school. I was trained on the old six-pack of trusty instruments that kept the dirty side down with confidence and reliable comfort for years. Never was I in doubt of them saving my hide, even when I had to go partial panel a couple of times in real weather. Surely almost every other instrument-rated pilot and CFII who has flown in a cloud will agree it would take a big leap of faith to put our trust into a comp;letely new type of technology. Being won over by high tech glass cockpits wasn't easy at first. Fortunately, skepticism isn't my middle name, because going from the round gauges to flat glass was easy for me.

What is the difference between trusting glass displays versus the old analog gauges in real IMC? I have to know that whatever I replace the only true horizon with must be a reliable substitute. It takes about eight seconds for us to lose the real horizon reference if we don't have a reliable replacement source to rely on. That's not much more than several blinks of an eye. Without total trust in the instrument display, a pilot will have doubts about the information that they provide. These doubts are eliminated only after several hours of flying behind a primary flight display (PFD).

The large PFD provides immediate feedback as to what the aircraft is doing without reaching the outer limits of one's peripheral vision. This means your scan isn't quite as sweeping. The color horizon is crisp and clean, which made this the easiest part of the transition for me. Finding the location of information that is traditionally presented by round gauges is the more challenging aspect. The AI is still substituted in the middle of your scan, but the supporting information that is typically provided by the other five primaries for keeping things glued is slightly different. The displays show altitude and airspeed on both a tape and corresponding digital readout, and VSI has more of the traditional needle scale look, with an up or down movement in an arched scale display. Fortunately, all of this is extremely easy to adapt to with little transition effort.

One of the first questions from many old-school pilots is how readable is an all glass aircraft during bright daylight? Typically any glass display that is now in production is fully readable in any type of lighting condition, including bright sunlight. Most pilots even find that they are more concerned with a nighttime situation when they must turn down the intensity. However, angular viewing can be a problem on some of the single multi-use glass displays. This doesn't pose a problem for the left seat pilot, but the instructor in the left seat can have a problem unless he or she moves his or her head to the left almost 45 degrees to get a clear picture of what the aircraft is doing.

An area that gives many pilots the initial fear of using a glass display aircraft is in learning the toggle button and knob routines. Again, the manufacturers have done a great job of making the design easy to adapt to. It still might take longer to fully provide the comfort zone of the traditional instrument panel, but glass provides a more comprehensive list of options. It is well worth the effort to learn the operation by use of the software programs that all of the manufacturers of glass avionics offer. A couple of hours of dual ground instruction using this software can save many tense moments in the aircraft, especially when doing missed approaches and other flight operations that require confidence in operational tasks.

Teaching tasks such as constant-speed climbs and descents from a PFD has a more disciplined approach than with the traditional instrument setup. Power is still the first adjustment to be made in either case. However, setting up the climb or descent on the graphic display requires a stricter adherence to holding the predetermined climb or descent angle. The horizon display has a much broader display background so it is more sensitive to control inputs. Holds can be somewhat easier to teach using the MFD. The larger display requires less head down time. Use of the Garmin 430 OBS button after executing the missed approach puts the published hold directly over the fix or intersection.

I switch between glass cockpits and traditional flight instruments all the time, and the adjustment is not really that noticeable, but you still need to be current and need to consider your personal weather minimums when flying either type aircraft.

8

INCORPORATING THE DESKTOP SIMULATOR INTO FLIGHT TRAINING CURRICULUMS

...They all needed to obtain their instrument rating in the most effective and efficient manner...and the desktop flight simulator played a crucial role in the success of their training.

INSTRUMENT TRAINING METHODS

Grueling. That is what some pilots have said about the accelerated instrument training programs offered from flight training establishments throughout the country. Some of these instrument-trained pilots have written about their experiences in flight publications and magazines. I am going to tell you the other side of the experience from the perspective of the instrument flight instructor. This chapter will highlight how the desktop flight simulator can augment a flight training syllabus, especially when conducted in an accelerated training program.

In November 1995, I continued my lengthy flight instructor career by subcontracting my services to a company specializing in accelerated training courses. The company has been in the business of training pilots for their instrument ratings for over 25 years. After being accepted as a potential member of the flight instructor staff, you must attend and pass the one week indoctrination course.

This training program has proven that a desktop flight simulator can be successfully integrated into an instrument training syllabus. The ground portion of this company's course is built around the successful textbook, *The Instrument Flight Training Manual* by Peter Dogan. This book is still considered a good source for information on instrument flying.

I subcontracted as a flight instructor until August 2000 when I decided to work independently. Having signed off many instrument pilot applicants, I designed my own program based on my experience and work with FTDs and PCATDs.

Over the years of teaching, I have picked up some training tips I'd like to share, along with some of the assignments I experienced while helping clients overcome the obstacles in their training. The training victims, as I sometimes referred to them, included doctors, lawyers, TV personalities and various other high profile individuals. They all needed to obtain their instrument rating in the most effective and efficient manner, and the accelerated training program was the obvious choice for accomplishing that task. The desktop flight simulator played a crucial role in their training success.

Accelerated vs. Non-Accelerated Training

I can speak from both sides of the flight training spectrum when I say I know the advantages and disadvantages of accelerated vs. traditional training. Prior to conducting accelerated instrument programs, I had graduated many students who took traditional instrument training at my FAA-approved flight school in Michigan. These graduates went on to become proficient and competent pilots. The Michigan weather can be a challenging environment for flying, but it is important for instructors to meet with students on a consistent and regular basis, regardless of the weather. Twice a week is an ideal training schedule. In the meantime, the desktop flight simulator can provide valuable training when the weather does not cooperate.

Students I have trained using the accelerated curriculum programs have also gone on to become proficient and competent pilots. One problem that arises with intensive training is the mental and physical fatigue. Some people have trouble coping with it, so it's important that each person evaluate their own tolerance level before committing to a rigorous training schedule.

Some flight instructors do not believe an instrument student can absorb that much training in a compressed timeframe. They do not believe that you can train a competent instrument pilot in ten days, and that it is more likely you will produce an applicant who can simply pass the exam. This thinking is shortsighted. The military has trained their pilots for years using accelerated programs, and the airlines require their crews to train in short intensive programs.

Statistics show that the average instrument pilot earns his rating in about 65 hours of training. A concentrated training program can shorten this to 40 or 50 hours. Part of this time can be spent in an approved ground trainer, so the cost savings can be significant. In addition, piece-meal instruction can result in more than one instructor, which raises the cost of training.

Instrument training in glass panel TAA requires more time, so some pilots who own advanced system aircraft opt to take their IFR training in a basic instrument trainer to earn their instrument wings, and then transition to their TAA.

Training in IMC is more likely to happen within ten *continuous* days. Some of my clients/students have spent most of their training time in the clouds and have been more comfortable and better prepared, on the day of the checkride, to fly real weather in the IFR system.

I favor the ten-day program for students who have some previous instrument experience and are completely committed and focused on the program.

The Roaming CFII

Imagine meeting someone for the first time and spending the next ten to 12 days teaching them the intricacies of instrument flying. Amplify the situation by considering you are together in what has been described as the smallest classroom in the world! This is the life of an instrument instructor who travels from one client to another, conducting accelerated instrument training. It can take place at any time, in any place in the country. Whoever teaches these programs lives, eats and breathes instrument flying for eight hours a day. But the thread that binds you with your student from day one is your common interest: flying. Even though personality differences can surface, I have found that we learn to tolerate each other throughout the training.

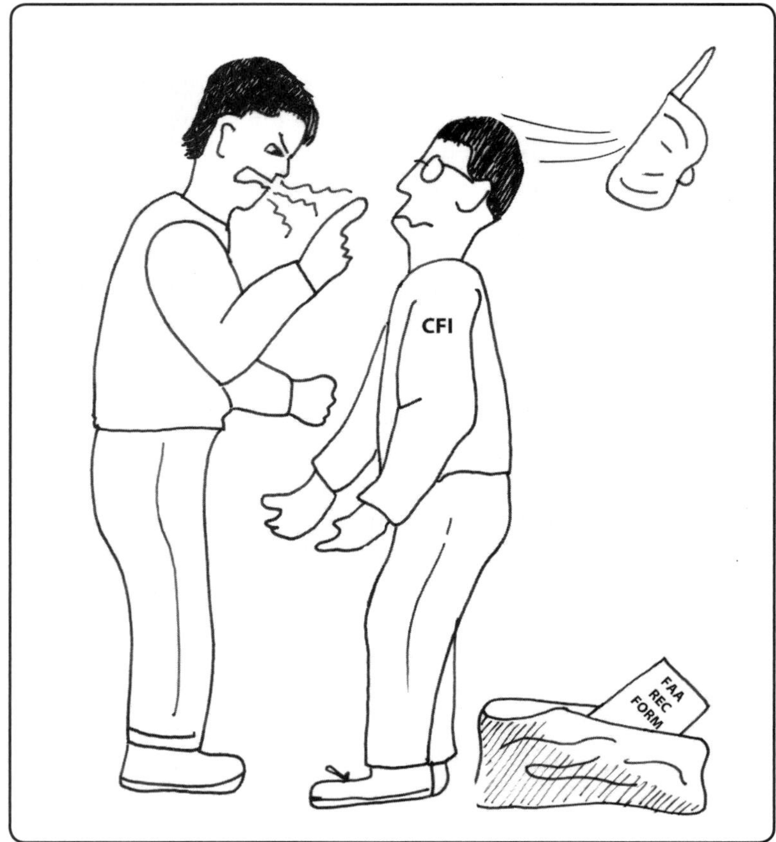

Sometimes there are personality differences.

Preparing a Client Prior to the First Lesson

When integrating a desktop flight simulator into your training syllabus, suggest to your students that they get a head start by purchasing flight simulator software and a simple joystick to practice basic instrument flight assignments at home. The following are some practice items I tell them to work on prior to our first session in the aircraft:

Objective: For the student to learn scanning techniques and become familiar with the operating characteristics of the desktop flight simulator.

Content:

- Select your own personal aircraft and instrument layout from the list that most closely matches your aircraft's configuration.
- Position the aircraft over the closest local VOR station at 2,000 feet on a heading of 360 degrees.
- Configure all the avionics as appropriate for the local tower and navigation stations.
- Start by flying straight and level and holding heading within 10 degrees and altitude within 100 feet.
- After fifteen minutes of practice, make several 90-degree turns.
- Follow this exercise by doing several 180 degree turns.
- Next, do several 360 degree turns.
- Climb and level off at 3,000 feet.
- Descend and level off at 2,000 feet.
- Execute a 90-degree climbing turn to 3,000 feet.
- Execute a 90-degree descending turn to 2,000 feet.
- If after practicing the above exercises, and heading and altitude control are within the limits to a consistent level of performance, begin the next exercise.
- Track outbound on any cardinal point radial for ten miles and keep CDI within one quarter scale and altitude within 100 feet.
- Reverse course with a 180-degree heading and track back to the VOR. After station passage, track outbound on another radial and repeat the process.

Completion Standards: This exercise is complete when the student can perform straight and level, turns, climbs and descents to within specified limits. The exercise is complete when the student is able to consistently perform the tracking limits.

Recommended Reading: FAA *Instrument Flying Handbook* Chapters 1 and 2.

Note: This assignment can be emailed to your client. Suggest they call or email you with any questions regarding setup or operation of the desktop flight simulator. These procedures provide a way for you to evaluate how serious your student is about the training. Include such information as required books, hours to be flown, cost of training, availability of your time, etc.

Giving this simple syllabus to a potential flight student will demonstrate how serious they are regarding the training; it also helps them be more prepared for the first lesson in the aircraft.

Lessons Learned from Two Training Assignments

The following are training assignments I completed with two clients. I'm sharing these as a way to convey some of the factors involved with instrument training using a desktop flight simulator. I have changed the names of the clients.

Students learn from the mistakes of others. Each training assignment can mentally put you in the right seat of an aircraft or desktop flight simulator and allow you visualize the situation as it plays out.

The stories start out with the location and a brief personal background of the client. Each covers the difficulties that crop up, followed by a wrap-up and conclusion. I believe after reading these assignment situations, you will realize how the use of the desktop flight simulator filled the gaps between flying and ground time and helped each client pass his or her checkride successfully.

Marion, Indiana

Bill lived in Marion, Indiana. He had a Cherokee Six 300. His training sessions with me would complete his training program based on the 20–30 hours of instrument time in his logbook. Bill's father had been providing right seat safety time to build up his hood time.

I called Bill after arriving at the hotel in Marion. I met him at his office the next morning, and we set up the desktop flight simulator in a room he had prepared for the training period. After some basic instruction, I realized Bill had a good touch on the trainer. What he lacked was knowledge of the IFR material, which he would need to know for the practical test.

We took a quick trip to Bill's hangar, and I checked the paperwork for his aircraft to ensure no glitches would crop up later. I was impressed with his airplane. It was well equipped, including a Stormscope and autopilot. The turbocharged engine added extra performance. We flew for a couple of hours. I observed his good command of the aircraft, but realized we would need to work on his scanning skills.

After an afternoon of evaluation, I told Bill it was possible we could complete his training in three to four days. Little did I realize how the weather would affect that goal.

That evening I awoke to the sound of 50-knot winds that almost blew out one of my hotel windows, but I figured we could still start with some heavy ground training in the morning until the winds subsided and then log a few hours in the aircraft later in the day.

However, we were grounded for the next two days, so we spent quality time in the books and practicing on the desktop flight simulator all the tasks we would need to eventually accomplish in the aircraft. We practiced all the air work maneuvers for the checkride and the cross-country flight we would do in the aircraft. I played ATC and the weather briefer, and Bill seemed to have his doubts whether this would be valuable training, but his scanning skills continued to improve. This would be important when we shifted his focus back to the aircraft.

Finally, on the third day the weather cooperated, and it was evident the time remaining would be spent dedicated to flying the aircraft. I could tell Bill welcomed the change. With the combined approved hours on the desktop simulator and those in the aircraft, Bill would still be at the minimum requirements to complete his instrument rating.

Our long instrument cross-country was a flight to Champaign, Illinois. This was the one required area that had to be completed in the aircraft. Bill performed well and had improved his scanning skills. By the end of day three, I checked his logbook and conducted a quick review of his ground knowledge to be sure he was ready for the checkride.

I then gave him a mock checkride on the desktop flight simulator. He did extremely well. Another front was moving into the Marion area, which didn't look at all favorable for the morning checkride. I decided to sign him off and leave for home. My normal procedure is to be present and lend my client support during the day of the checkride, but it was apparent I should leave before the storm arrived.

I gave Bill a signed recommendation form, wished him good luck, and hoped the weather would improve so he could schedule another checkride.

Acceptable weather finally worked its way into the area and Bill took his checkride. He passed and was awarded his instrument rating. He called to thank me for the training and mentioned his fondness for the desktop flight simulator.

Important aspects of Bill's training: How often has weather been a factor that not only kept you from flying with a student, but also caused you to lose out on an opportunity to get paid for your time? Bill was able to get through what could have been a disappointing training experience had we not taken advantage of quality ground instruction interspersed with desktop flight training.

Pentwater, Michigan

Patty was located in Pentwater, MI, which is located just south of Ludington. It's a lovely resort village that harbors many boats and is a summer residence for some influential people. My client, Patty, was 19 years old and a college student on break for the summer. Although from Virginia, her family had a vacation home nestled deep in the woods on the Lake Michigan shoreline. Patty was to train in the family's Cherokee PA-28-235. We had planned a full ten-day instrument training program.

I called several days before my appointed arrival time to confirm we would be working together. When I spoke to her, I had the impression Patty was younger than 19. It would be the first time I had trained such a young person for an instrument rating utilizing a desktop flight simulator incorporating the accelerated method.

When we met, she was as I had expected—young and shy. She was dressed in the typical teenage attire, i.e., blue jeans and sweatshirt. Patty was eager to get started, so we sat down and discussed the instrument training program by reviewing her logbook. We began to check out the aircraft paperwork, and as I was setting up the desktop flight simulator, she told me she had soloed at 16 and received her private pilot license on her 17th birthday. Her logbook showed she had accumulated about 25 hours of instrument instruction, about 8 hours in actual IMC.

We spent the first morning training on the desktop flight simulator. I was glad to see the delicate touch Patty had on the controls and her scanning skills. When we flew the aircraft in the afternoon, it was apparent that she had great piloting skills.

After several days of training, when I began to introduce holding techniques, Patty hit a mental block. When we moved further into instrument approach procedures, more cobwebs began to clog her brain.

We spent the next full day going step-by-step through each of these problem areas until I knew it was time to migrate back to the aircraft. On the fifth day, we shifted our focus back to the aircraft, and everything started to click for her.

A good instrument pilot needs to have positional awareness at any given time, and that skill can be practiced on the desktop flight simulator. Holding practice and the rigors of doing many course reversal turns while doing instrument approaches are easily practiced on the simulator.

The rest of Patty's training continued without difficulty. Her Dad was present for her checkride and nervously waited for the results. The examiner told me Patty performed one of the best checkrides he had ever seen.

Important aspects of Patty's training: Had Patty not encountered a problem with positional awareness in the aircraft, she would have been a rare student. It is one of the most difficult traits to teach. Using a desktop flight simulator makes this part of the instrument training process less stressful and more meaningful. Once it is grasped on the ground in a more relaxed setting, my clients seem to learn faster and experience less anxiety in an aircraft. Patty told me she was going to purchase her own desktop flight simulator to sharpen her proficiency. Even her instrument-rated father was impressed with the way it helped her overcome the training rough spots.

Transferring Lessons Learned on the Desktop Simulator to the Aircraft

The desktop flight simulator should be used to teach the lessons, while the aircraft is where the practice and practical use occur. Your flight students will understand and appreciate this as you progress through the syllabus with them.

There are two syllabi in the Appendix of this book: a *Private Pilot BATD Syllabus* and an *Instrument Rating PCATD Syllabus*. These syllabi illustrate the value in correlating the ground lessons from the desktop flight simulator with flying sessions in the aircraft. The lessons include the tasks that are the most difficult to teach with the help of a flight simulator, including holding patterns, DME arcs, intercepting and tracking NAVAIDs, and instrument approaches. Forming a mental picture of these exercises in an aircraft can challenge any new student learning instrument procedures. Therefore in this aspect the desktop flight simulator makes the ideal teaching tool. Use it to demonstrate the maneuver, show the student the map of the lesson flown, and then have the student perform the procedure. Vary the conditions until you see the student has a firm mental picture of the maneuver.

Flight Maneuvers that Should ***Not*** Be Taught on the Desktop Flight Simulator

There are two flight maneuvers that cannot be practically taught on the desktop flight simulator: recovery from unusual attitudes and steep turns. Both maneuvers should be reserved for demonstration and practice in the actual aircraft used for training. You can describe and discuss the techniques while sitting in front of the simulator, but the actual feel and sensation experienced while performing the maneuvers in the aircraft cannot be generated on a standard desktop flight simulator.

You can use the simulator to simulate instrument failure in the aircraft by clicking on the center of the instrument face to cover it up. This has the same effect as placing a "soap cover" over the instrument face in the aircraft. The student can then proceed to the steps for recovering from an unusual attitude, such as those that will take place in the aircraft. Otherwise, both the unusual attitude and steep turn tasks are best reserved for the aircraft.

Neither is the simulator the place to practice or demonstrate takeoffs and landings. These maneuvers require physical fidelity not available from a desktop flight simulator. While it's okay to demonstrate the associated tasks that take place during these phases of flight, it's best to judge a student's performance while in flight.

Preflight and Postflight Simulator Applications

Using the desktop flight simulator to introduce a flight task or procedure, and again as a review, provides maximum learning opportunity to support inflight activities. The postflight discussion can lead to another brief review with some dual demo and practice on the simulator.

It would also be beneficial to have the student do solo practice at home with their own personal hardware/software. This will further enhance the learning process as each stage of the syllabus is completed.

9

SIMULATING WEATHER

...Remember, pilots should not dread weather, they should respect it.

WEATHER WISDOM

There is a better way than going airborne to teach your student how to use good judgment when it comes to making good weather decisions. That method is the desktop flight simulator.

As flight instructors, we all realize weather is one of the most hazardous aspects of learning to fly. With a desktop flight simulator, you can set weather parameters that can be programmed to change as the flight lesson progresses. You can even program in the current weather conditions at your home base and execute an approach right down to minimums before taking on the actual challenge in an aircraft. The desktop flight simulator can elevate the discussions you had on weather with your students to practical decision making on their part. You can effectively evaluate how they will react. It's a fantastic tool instructors can use to truly test a student's judgment and inflight decision making skills before heading to the tarmac.

Because weather is a constantly-changing phenomenon that needs to be considered and monitored prior to and during every flight, you need to provide a flexible learning environment for your student. Yet it's a difficult subject to assess a pilot's skill, short of watching the decisions play out, which is why desktop flight simulators are particularly useful.

You need to teach students how to make informed decisions based on weather reports from several sources. If it appears the weather is going to be unfavorable for flight, the pilot must be firm in her no-go decision and not let any outside influences pressure her otherwise.

In instrument flying, the margins of safety are tighter for decision making just as they are for performance. This makes a go/no-go assessment more complex, as the decision must take into account the individual's limitations.

There are four basic weather conditions to consider when teaching your students how to make a go/no-go assessment: 1) widespread fog at the destination airport; 2) unavoidable thunderstorms; 3) icing conditions forecasted at the altitudes you have to fly; and 4) unusually high or gusty winds. Some pilots may feel that one or several of these factors are acceptable for flying based upon the aircraft's capability and the skill of the pilot, but in my experience, judgment dictates that if one or more of these four factors are present, I stay on the ground, and that's what I teach my students.

There is a natural human trait called self-preservation. I call it the "warm and fuzzy feeling." Encourage your students to develop this sense: If they don't have a warm and fuzzy feeling about the weather forecast, they shouldn't go up. It has saved many pilots from flying in conditions that could have resulted in a serious accident. Experience, knowledge and equipment all play an important part in helping the pilot tune into this natural awareness. It is rare, but there are some pilots who seem destined to disaster because they shun this natural trait and take chances with the weather. These are often the ones we read about later in accident reports and newspapers. I have lost some close friends to weather-related accidents, so I know how painful it is to try to figure out why they decided to fly when they did. Share your personal weather experiences with your students, not with the intention to scare them, but instead to make them aware of the pitfalls of poor judgment when dealing with weather decisions.

Weather theory can be boring for students, but it is a necessary and vital part of learning to fly. It can be made more interesting and fun by using the desktop flight simulator. My goal in this chapter is to provide you, the instructor, with practical guidance in using the desktop flight simulator to transfer your weather knowledge to your students.

Obtain Accurate Weather Information

No doubt about it, a brief look out a window provides the first clue as to what your student can expect for local conditions prior to going to the airport. Describe cloud formations and teach them how to quickly scan the sky to form the key observations they will need before calling the briefer.

Today's weather forecasting is so much more accurate than it was even several years ago. When I started flying in the mid-1960s, there was a 50/50 chance the weather forecast you got would be correct. With the technology we have now, weather forecasting is closer to 85–90% accurate. Over the past few years, I have rarely had unforecasted weather pop up on a flight. The only exception might have been some unforecasted or unreported inflight icing that didn't present a serious problem.

Even though I use and appreciate the many computer-based programs that enable me to access weather information and file a flight plan on my PC, I like to talk to a weather briefer. This is especially important if our instructional flights will involve flying approaches to minimums. The people in the Flight Service Station (FSS) are trained to interpret weather reports and make qualified suggestions based on their knowledge. Although it's possible that briefers may disappear as the FAA phases out the few remaining stations that still exist, they are currently available, so tell your students to make good use of them.

Whatever method you use to teach your clients or students, tell them it is necessary to monitor the sky for any change that might occur if flying in VMC. I teach them that a change in wind direction is a good indicator of impending weather changes that may not have been anticipated in the forecast.

I do most of my flight instruction in Florida. The heat can be quite uncomfortable in the summer, and it is easy to get dehydrated. I plan my instructional flights either early in the morning or later in the evening when it is cooler, less humid and therefore less stressful.

Teach Decisiveness

Tell your clients and students they should never ask a briefer to make a go/no-go decision for them. Most briefers are not trained as pilots and should not be expected to make such a decision. Teach your students that they are the pilot-in-command of the aircraft and have the final say as to whether they should fly, based on the information they receive from weather reports and forecasts. This is not to say that the briefer cannot provide guidance or give her or his opinion about what to expect. They definitely are trained to read the reports and interpret the weather charts, but they cannot make that final decision and do not want to be put in that position.

Once you have gathered all the necessary information to make the go/no-go choice based on the forecast data, you need to be decisive. There is nothing worse than having unsettling reservations about your decision. You need to establish clear-cut parameters based on your personal minimums. These can vary with experience. If you have any nagging concerns about the weather and your comfort level for flying in it, you should take a step back and reconsider. *Do not allow outside pressure to affect your decision.* However, if you can make a decision with a clear conscience, you need to stick to that assessment with confidence and let the cards fall where they may. Your passengers will surely sense uneasiness if you are uncomfortable with your decision, so get a firm grip on your comfort zone. It's your first major course of action as a pilot.

If the weather gets worse, every pilot should have an escape plan. The alternate airport, if required, is only part of that plan. The overall weather decision should be to pick an appropriate alternate that fits into a "what if" list of scenarios.

Remember: Pilots should not dread weather, they should respect it. In reality, during most of the nontransitional seasons of the year, the weather is generally VFR.

WEATHER CONDITIONS

Wind

The earth we fly over can tell us a lot about the weather if we make some basic observations. Until I took my seaplane training, I had little perception of how a smooth lake or body of water can provide information about the wind. If you watch the streaks on the surface of a smooth lake, you can tell the direction of the wind. A rough estimate of wind speed can be determined by observing the length and intensity of the streaks. This pertains to VFR operations, of course, but it is one more telltale sign to keep pilots up to date on the ever changing conditions. Wind knowledge is an essential part of flying.

When setting up the simulator, plug in some strong variance in the wind direction and speed. This will let you see how your student responds and will provide an opportunity to discuss wind corrections, and even more importantly, detecting wind.

Ice

There aren't many general aviation aircraft that are certified to fly in known icing conditions. Icing conditions are probably one of the hardest weather hazards to predict, and pilot reports are one of the most important ways to learn about them, as they can warn you about what altitudes to avoid.

You need to report to ATC at the slightest indication of ice formation. You are not in violation of FAA regulation simply because you are picking up a slight amount of ice, but this condition does mean you need to begin your escape plan.

One form of ice that pilots seem to ignore is frost. When I had my flight school in Detroit, there were several times when I saw a pilot on the ramp polishing the leading edges of the frosted wings to get ready to fly. We use the term "polishing" to describe what someone does when they wipe a dry towel over the wing surface to remove the frost that has formed overnight. The friction from rubbing can heat the surface enough to remove a light covering of frost, especially if the air temperature is close to freezing. But this is not a safe practice, even though pilots may think this will make the aircraft airworthy. Although I never saw a plane fail to take off after this procedure, it is still a foolhardy practice.

Although you can't simulate icing conditions in desktop flight simulators, you can teach students to look for the likely causes. You can set up weather conditions that test their recognition of icing at both the surface and altitude.

Wind Shear and Turbulence

Most instrument pilots would probably tell you they would rather fly in low IFR that is smooth than in turbulent IMC. Nothing is more nerve-wracking than to be bouncing around in an aircraft, trying to hold altitude and heading, while tuning radios and completing other cockpit-related tasks. It's all part of instrument flying, but it is the least pleasant part of flying in the weather. If you throw in low-level wind shear and an approach to minimums, pilots are in for one of the most challenging and adrenaline producing conditions. Split-second reflexes and sweaty palms are to be expected when coping with these situations, but any instrument pilot worth her salt will confess she has conquered many of these artful dances in the air.

I have sat in the back of airliners that made these tough approaches and could almost feel the flow of energy from the front office of the aircraft as the crew made some fairly wild control inputs. I clearly remember one flight to Las Vegas when the aircraft was being buffeted around on final. I was relieved to finally feel the surge of power for the go-around once the pilot realized the wind shear was just too much to handle. I bet it was one night the flight crew was glad to get safely on the ground.

Be sure to simulate turbulent conditions at all altitudes in the desktop simulator, prior to taking the student up in these conditions. The desktop simulator is a better classroom when talking about the necessities of holding attitude, rather than altitude, when bouncing around in the soup.

Thunderstorms

Flying where I do in Florida, thunderstorms occur almost daily in summer months. You can pretty much predict active thunderstorms every afternoon around three o'clock. There is so much moisture in the air that the daily heat creates huge buildups. Some of these can rise to extreme upper levels of the atmosphere before they finally cause severe storms with heavy rain, high winds and hail.

Every pilot knows that thunderstorms should be avoided. Flying with weather-avoidance equipment on an aircraft helps to circumnavigate these storms with more confidence. Regardless, most Florida pilots give thunderstorms the respect they deserve.

One time I was flying a Cessna 210 on a charter flight with freight. I was on my way back to Detroit City Airport from Youngstown, Ohio and was in instrument conditions from the time I left the ground. There was reported weather, but nothing severe enough to keep me from making the flight. The sky was getting blacker and blacker from the moisture-laden clouds, and the rain was getting more intense. I asked ATC if they could give me any information about the weather ahead, but this was in the early seventies, and they had no weather radar capability back then. All they could report was some heavy echoes on their radar scopes. By then it was too late.

Soon I could hear the heavy beating of hail on the windscreen of the aircraft. Any pilot who has flown in and around thunderstorms can tell you there is nothing more disconcerting than trying to speculate how much hail can break an aircraft's windscreen. This is one of those situations when you know you shouldn't be there, but you are and have to deal with it, so you fly the airplane and hope for the best.

Fortunately, after a few miles I was out of the most severe part of the storm and relieved that the hail had subsided. I remember thinking I did not want to ever feel that vulnerable again and would do anything I could to avoid it. It was one time when the weather was worse than predicted, but flying is about learning by experience, and those experiences often reinforce the notion that it's not worth taking chances with weather.

One way to teach this lesson in a safer environment is to simulate various weather fronts; weather recognition is half the feat in avoiding severe weather. Use the desktop simulator to plug in various weather conditions, and then ask your student what they think they might encounter in the air.

Fog

Probably one of the most insidious weather hazards is fog. One night I almost became a statistic because of it, and I am lucky to be around to talk about it. Fog can occur whenever the temperature and dew point reach the same value. Whenever the spread is within a few degrees between the temperature and dew point, pilots need to take notice. In my experience, this is one of the least accurate predictions a weather briefer can make, even with today's high tech equipment.

Keeping close tabs on the temperature/dew point spread is therefore one of a pilot's first weather priorities. When conditions are right for fog to form, it can occur with hardly any warning. Ground fog can keep us grounded with widespread weather below minimums.

The only good thing about flying in and around fog is that the air is typically smooth. There is very little turbulence, and an aircraft can land on most any runway if the conditions are not below minimums for the approach. This, however, was a contributing factor in the death of a friend who was doing a circle-to-land approach, at night, at an airport in Canada with heavy ground fog. The accident occurred on a charter flight with the weather just above minimums for the approach. He apparently caught sight of the ground for a moment, and then got below minimums during the circling maneuver.

The young pilot with him was also killed in the crash. The accident investigators found him in the cockpit the next morning with his right hand still on the throttles, apparently trying to climb and get altitude. Obviously it was a wasted effort, but the desire to survive was paramount up to the moment of impact.

Today, most charter and passenger carriers state in their operations procedures that nonprecision circle-to-land approaches cannot be conducted at night. This makes good sense when you consider the hazards of this type of operation. I have used this scenario on the PCATD to see how well students do; frequently their decisions result in what would be a fatal accident!

Sideline Point of Interest:
Use George, Your Faithful Autopilot in Weather

If you have an autopilot in your aircraft but haven't been using it to its full potential, especially when flying in IMC, you are not using good judgment. When you use the autopilot, you still have to keep your scan up on the primary flight instruments, but an autopilot allows you to handle other tasks in the cockpit while concentrating on the flight instruments. This is especially true in bad weather, when a pilot needs to reserve his mental alertness and reduce stress as he prepares for the final approach and landing.

A good autopilot is probably one of the key avionics components when it comes to cockpit resource management. Having "George" as your right-hand man means you can relax a little when you are boring a straight line between fixes, or getting a new vector to a waypoint or airport. You can let him fly while you get out the next approach chart, change fuel tanks, tune the radios, watch for traffic, or even do a little sightseeing.

10

IMPLEMENTING YOUR OWN PLAN OF ACTION

"FLYING" THE DESKTOP FLIGHT SIMULATOR WITH YOUR STUDENT

I have covered a lot of airspace with techniques for using a desktop flight simulator for flight training. Now I want to give you specific "meat" for putting together a viable and comprehensive training program that will be meaningful to both you and your client base.

Let's start off with tips you can pass on to your students. A skilled instrument flight instructor has the ability to transfer his knowledge to a willing learner who wants to become an accomplished instrument pilot. To do this, you need to have a structured plan of action and valuable tips you can pass on to your fledglings. I will lay out a plan for you to use, but first I will cover the tips that will help you in this process.

By now you have the background knowledge and incentive to consider purchasing and using a desktop flight simulator. However, before you spend the money, you need to do your homework. Consider your personal situation. Do you have the time and space it will take to set up and learn a simulator? Are you really sold on the idea that a simulator will enhance the bag of tools you already use in your flight training? Remember what I told you in Chapter Five: As an instructor, you need to be totally convinced that the desktop flight simulator is a solid and valuable tool to use with your students. If you are convinced, then read on. The following sections will help get you going.

TIPS FOR USING THE ON TOP FLIGHT SIMULATOR

The following tips are mostly specific to the On Top software. I don't suggest presenting these to your clients during the first lesson. Rather, I suggest you introduce them as more dual time is spent on the simulator and the tips become more applicable.

General instructing tips with desktop flight simulators:

Change the settings. Just like in the real plane, you won't do your students any favors by leaving cockpit and avionics settings where they should to be.

- Between flights and approaches, test your students' use of checklists and procedures by "deselecting" settings, such as the marker beacon, DME setting, ADF frequency, etc. (Note: see the upcoming tip on Radio Phraseology for more detail.)

V_1 Cuts

The minimum amount of time that can be programmed for an engine failure is one minute. Therefore, the best way to program a V_1 cut is to select 1 minute for the failure delay and then sit on the ground for a period of about 20 or 30 seconds before starting the takeoff roll. Experiment with a few takeoffs to figure out which time delay works best for what you want to accomplish.

Note about using MAP mode:

When you click on **SETUP** during a flight, it resets the starting point for the flight tracking you see in **MAP** mode. In other words, every time you click on **SETUP**, the track of the flight you are on will be erased. However, by toggling straight to **MAP** from the cockpit menu, the flight track will remain continuous, and you can go back and forth to the **MAP** without losing any of the saved flight track data.

- **Reset after a crash.** Three things will cause you to get a crash screen in On Top: Excessive bank, excessive descent rate, or landing gear selected up when the airplane contacts the ground. If you get the crash screen, you may have to reset the condition that caused the crash before getting airborne again. You cannot just click reset if the plane "landed" with 50 degrees of bank. In such a case, you need to click on **SETUP** and reset the pitch, bank or gear before flying again.

How to Do a Quick Set Up

Sometimes you may want to do a quick reposition to a runway or point in space and have no file saved for that position. Here are two options.

To start at the end of a runway:

1. Click **Setup**; **Position**; select the airport ID and click **GO** under set WPT.
2. On the **Slew map** in the upper right corner click 4 times on **Slew In**.
3. Click and drag the airplane to the end of the runway you want to fly from; click **Slew In** once more and center the airplane on the runway.
4. In the lower right corner select the heading and altitude you want to start the flight. The fastest way is with your keyboard.

Click on the black box under **Hdg /Alt**. When it turns gray you can clear the old number with the backspace key; then type in the new number you want. To set that figure, click the gray box and it will turn black again.

5. The program knows where the field elevation is; a quick way to set field elevation is to click the decrease **Alt** button until the altitude bottoms out. This is your field elevation.
6. If you want to auto-tune a frequency for navigation, click on the **navaid** symbol on the map, then choose **nav 1** or **nav 2**. Localizers are shown with a blue dot at the far end of the runway. Click on the blue dot to select the inbound heading and frequency.
7. Generally you want to start from a standstill. To set airspeed to zero, click on **Aircraft** and then scroll the airspeed down or backspace with the keyboard as before.
8. This is a good place to check that the gear is down. Check the first setting under the **Controls** column.
9. If you want to save this configuration, click **save setup** and give the file a name.
10. Click **SET** once all the parameters are set and you're back in the cockpit.

To start a flight from a point in space:

1. Click **Setup**; **Position**; select an airport ID, VOR or NDB and click GO under set WPT.
2. Click and drag the airplane to a point where you want to start the flight.
3. In the lower right corner select the heading and altitude you want. The fastest way is with your keyboard. Click on the black box under **Hdg /Alt**. When it turns gray you can clear the old number with the backspace key and type in the new number you want. To set that figure, click the gray box and it will turn black again.
4. If you want to auto-tune a frequency for navigation, click on the **navaid** symbol on the map, then choose **nav 1**, **nav 2** or **ADF**. Localizers are shown with a blue dot at the far end of the runway. Click on the blue dot to select the inbound heading and frequency.
5. To configure other settings such as airspeed click on **Aircraft** and select the aircraft conditions you want to start the flight with. Likewise you can select **Weather**, **Failures** etc.
6. If you want to save the flight in your library of scenarios, click **save setup** and give the file a name.

Navigation Database

The navigation database in On Top is updated with each new release of the software. Short of that, you may find that changes have occurred in your area that need updating.

Rather than have users subscribe to an update service, we have created an airspace editor that installs when you first load the program.

Details on using the editor are found in the On Top POH (user's manual). If you have questions about the interface, contact ASA tech support at: support@asa2fly.com or call (800) ASA-2FLY (272-2359)

Tips for Radio Phraseology

Whether flying in an aircraft or working with your student on the desktop flight simulator, tell him that talking on the radio is a skill that must be mastered while flying on an IFR flight plan. The old adage of, "aviate, navigate, and communicate" is true; however, if you don't understand and communicate properly on the radio, it is both unsafe and unprofessional. Let your student tune the avionics in a flight simulator just as you would in an aircraft, without interference from you.

Tell your student that ATC will know by the tone of his voice and manner, whether or not he is knowledgeable, experienced and confident. If he hesitates to acknowledge a heading or altitude change, or he fumbles a clearance, ATC will have to work him in with other faster traffic. What's more, if he doesn't know the proper phraseology to use when requesting a new routing or altitude, it can tie up the radio in high-density areas. Your students will get the best service from the controllers if they know what to say and how to say it.

Using the radio is one of the biggest fears for new instrument students. This is why clearance copying presents a big hurdle in the training if not properly taught. New pilots are afraid to make a mistake and have the whole world hear it!

I do a lot of practice clearance copying exercises by playing controller while the student plays pilot. This helps immensely in building confidence and developing one's own shorthand. I always stress there is no requirement to learn specific symbols or shorthand because this is a personal element and comes with experience. No one way is right or wrong.

Here are a few tips you can teach your students:

- Do not include zeroes in altitudes. It is a waste of time.

- Do not copy the destination or the aircraft number of the plane you are flying. One exception would be if the clearance limit is short of the destination.
- Give the clearance in sequence. It helps to remember the word CRAFT, (**C**learance limit, **R**outing, **A**ltitude, **F**requency, **T**ransponder).

I teach students that anytime they get a clearance, the only information the controller needs to be sure they have copied are the numbers. These numbers include altitudes, headings (include direction of turn), frequencies and transponder codes. Anything else is frivolous. Many times people get bogged down reading back a clearance because they are trying to include everything they heard. As instructors, we know this is unnecessary, so relay this to your instrument trainees early on.

Tell students to have pencil and paper ready when they contact clearance delivery for their clearance. Suggest they clear their minds of all extraneous thoughts, such as their daily schedule, etc. This prepares them for getting it right the first time on the readback.

A valuable experience for any trainee is to visit the local airport control tower and ATC facility. I try to do this with every instrument student with whom I work. It shows them up front that they are dealing with regular people who are there to help. It also helps them understand how the system works. I like to also include a bonus visit to the Flight Service Station, if there is one nearby. These steps can help keep "mic fright" from getting in the way of learning.

Tips for Communicating

Tell your students that if they are "cleared for the approach," they can go to the published altitudes and intercept the courses as specified on the approach plate. Students tend to get confused when they are told to intercept the final approach course, and fly it inbound. I teach that "cleared for the approach" are the magic words that allow a pilot to shoot the published approach. Make sure students ask the controller if they have any doubts about whether they are cleared, especially if intercepting the final approach course within ten miles of the airport.

Teach your trainees that establishing communication with ATC prior to entering Class B airspace is not the same as being cleared into Bravo airspace. Tell them that ATC must first state that the aircraft is cleared before it can enter the Class B airspace, unless the aircraft is operating on an IFR flight plan.

One great way for students to get a clearance at an uncontrolled airport is to use their cell phones. Calling on a cell phone means clearance void time can be less stressful, because you're ready to go and not rushing to prepare the aircraft for flight.

Note: Some of this material is based on an article I wrote for *IFR Magazine*.

Implementing the Plan

The following are three examples, demonstrated on the desktop trainer, of when to stay the course or make a turn.

First, give your student some background information about confusing scenarios an instrument pilot might face with an instrument flight plan. There are basically three scenarios that can cause this confusion. Describe in detail how they might play out in an aircraft. Then set each of them up on the desktop simulator using the following order:

Scenario #1: You're cleared for takeoff and told to turn to an assigned heading after departure. After getting some altitude, you contact departure control and report that you're airborne and climbing out on the tower-assigned heading.

Departure acknowledges you on the frequency and tells you that they have you in radar contact. No further instructions have been provided, and you can hear the controller is overloaded with traffic.

You're headed off course with the tower-assigned heading. How long do you have to maintain the assigned heading until you can make that turn to get on course to your destination?

How to implement this scenario using the desktop flight simulator: Role-play with your student. You take on the role of ATC. Don't tell them up front what they should do; just let them do what they feel is correct by turning or keeping the current heading and altitude. Position the aircraft on the runway and give them a tower clearance for takeoff and to maintain runway heading. After 500 feet, tell them to contact departure control. Offer no further instruction. After observation, discuss the correct action.

Correct Action: Tell your student the correct action is to stay on the assigned heading until cleared by ATC, even if the controller is bogged down with other traffic. ATC doesn't want or expect a pilot to make a turn from the tower-assigned heading until they can allow an on-course turn.

An aircraft heading is the result of an agreement struck between the tower and departure prior to the pilot's IFR release. The only overriding event is the loss of radio communications when IFR emergency rules would apply.

When departing from a nontowered airport that has a published departure procedure for obstacle or terrain clearance, a pilot should fly the published procedure. Often times these obscure textual departure procedures are overlooked.

Tell your student that he should fly the published departure procedure until he gets enough altitude to be in radar contact, and then expect the controlling radar facility to provide vectors on course.

Scenario #2: The enroute controller has just given you a turn off your current on-course heading. This heading is taking you at least 60 degrees off course.

There's little activity on the frequency. How long should you stay on this new course before you ask ATC for a turn back to heading that will take you to your destination?

How to implement this scenario using a desktop flight simulator: Role-play with your student. You take on the role of ATC. Don't tell them up front what they should do; just let them do what they feel is correct by turning or keeping the current heading and altitude. Position the aircraft near the local airport on an airway for a practice IFR flight plan and the MEA. Make initial contact and provide a vector to a course that is 60 degrees off the airway without a reason. After observation, discuss the correct action.

Correct Action: Tell your student that every time ATC provides vector from the current heading during an IFR flight, they must give the pilot a reason for the turn. If not, the pilot should ask. The reason may be because of traffic separation or spacing, to provide vectors for an approach, or for possible weather deviation.

If ATC provides no reason for the turn, it's considered to be a hole in the clearance. A hole means a void, which leaves open the question of what the pilot should expect to do in case there is loss of communication.

If a pilot gets a turn off course due to conflicting traffic and it seems like the frequency is dead, he might consider a query to ATC after a reasonable wait. It might seem like a lifetime before he gets a vector to get back on course, but he must not turn until ATC authorizes it.

If the pilot has a legitimate loss of communications, then he has to fly from his current position to his destination using the route clearance that he last received or had been asked to expect.

Scenario #3: You're told that this will be vectors for ILS 9 approach. You're vectored for the left base to a heading of 180° and are expecting one more vector to intercept the final approach course, but you see the localizer needle starting to move off from the full right side of the cage.

How to implement this scenario using a desktop flight simulator: Role-play with your student. You take on the role of ATC. Don't tell them up front what they should do; just let them do what they feel is correct by turning or keeping the current heading and altitude. Vector them for a local ILS approach and put them on base. Don't give any further instructions after you vector your student for the pass and watch the CDI needle move off center. After observation, discuss the correct action.

Correct Action: Ask your student how long they think they should wait before telling the radar controller they are passing through final. Instruct them to ask the person in the radar room. An exception would be if they were forewarned that ATC would be taking them through the final approach course for spacing.

Most of the time it won't happen, but it's best to suggest to the approach controller that you, the pilot, are beginning to see a half-scale deflection occur and haven't received an authorized turn to intercept.

Some lousy vectors can be provided, and apologies often are doled out if they have been forgotten about, but tell your student to speak up if there's a break on the frequency.

Now Get Motivated and Involved!

I hope this book has provided you with enough information to effectively use the desktop flight simulator sitting idle in your flight school office. If you haven't yet decided to purchase or use one in your flight training program, maybe you will now be inspired to make that purchase. The FAA recently introduced a Notice of Proposed Rulemaking (NPRM) that will further accredit the use of PCATD and FTD in training regimens; this far-reaching rule change will have students looking for instructors who utilize this beneficial technology. It's a good time to invest in the technology as more new products become available that can enhance the realism of your setup. If you desire an enclosure, there are several choices now available.

If you aren't already part of a flight instructor organization, I encourage you to consider joining NAFI or another flight instructor organization. Volunteering your time in your local FSDO safety programs will help get the word out that you have a desktop flight simulator available for training. Becoming an FAA Safety Team representative (called "FAAST" Representative, previously referred to as

FAA Safety Counselors) is not only a valuable use of your spare time, but a good way to establish yourself and further spread the word of your instructor talents.

Take time to visit the many websites that enable you to network with other flight instructors and flight schools that make use of desktop flight simulators in their training programs. These sites offer excellent support and technical tips that can make your ownership and use of a simulator more rewarding.

Remember to mention in your advertising literature and business cards that a desktop flight simulator is one of your training tools. It will help generate more business for you and your flight school.

Good luck and happy "flying"!

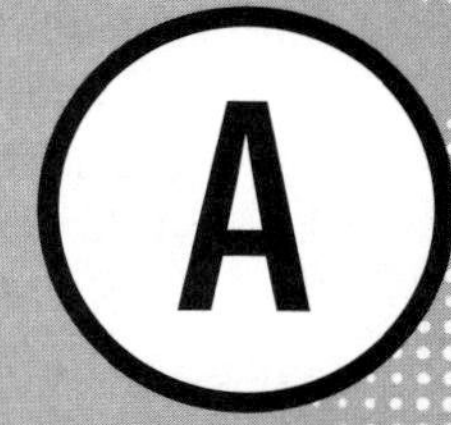

APPENDIX A: PRIVATE PILOT BASIC ATD SYLLABUS

PRIVATE PILOT SYLLABUS/ON TOP BASIC ATD

Course Objective

To supplement traditional flight training with improvements made possible with the On Top Basic ATD. Instructors are encouraged to use On Top creatively in producing scenario-based training that goes beyond the development of base motor skills.

Minimum Requirements

Flight instruction received with the On Top Basic ATD is loggable for Private Pilot training under Federal Aviation Regulations:

- 14 CFR 61.109 k)(1); **2.5 hours** towards the Private Pilot experience requirements.
- 14 CFR 141.57; any number of hours deemed appropriate by the school when conducting a special curricula dedicated to pilot proficiency.

Notes for Instructors

A Basic ATD or PCATD can effectively be integrated with ongoing training as a *supplemental* training tool.

Concepts are much easier to demonstrate and/or explain in a controlled and noiseless simulator environment. Take advantage of the *pause* button!

Flight schools can maximize the usefulness of the Basic ATD by leaving the unit on and accessible to instructors during periods of ongoing flight training. Instructors who can make free use of the device for specific discussions/skills development will maximize their students' training value. This is an inherent benefit to having computer based training available to the instructing staff.

Instructors should individually spend 2 to 3 hours apiece becoming familiar with the Basic ATD themselves in order to get comfortable with flight characteristics and functionality.

Important* Remember that primary students who do any flying in On Top will naturally tend to favor the gauges once they transition to an airplane. It is critical to employ integrated instruction techniques from the outset. Cover the airplane instrument panel if needed!

Use the following syllabus as a guide to implementing this technology with your overall training, but also as a starting point for even more diverse applications. There is no set limit to the usefulness of a Basic ATD in accomplishing your flight training objectives.

Lesson Placement

The following Modules may be supplemented using an approved Basic ATD in lieu of an airplane. The following Modules are suggested because the associated tasks and placement within the curriculum lend themselves particularly well to an integrated flight training environment:

Basic ATD Lesson	The Pilot's Manual: Private Pilot Syllabus	Lesson time
Lesson 1	Stage 1/Module 1	0.5 hr
Lesson 2	Stage 1/Module 3	0.5 hr
Lesson 3	Stage 1/Module 4	0.5 hr
Lesson 4	Stage 2/Module 3	0.5 hr
Lesson 5	Stage 2/Module 4	0.5 hr
Lesson 6	Stage 3/Module 1	0.5 hr
Lesson 7	Stage 3/Module 4	0.5 hr
Lesson 8	Stage 3/Module 3	0.5 hr

Total Loggable Time on Basic ATD: 2.5 hr

Specialized Flight Tasks—Optional Review

Objective: To utilize the Basic ATD environment to enhance specific flight skills.

While not comprehensive, this list is meant to offer instructors some suggestions on how to augment traditional instruction with the Basic ATD. Both instructors and students are encouraged to implement the device in ways that go beyond logging the hours.

Content:

Go-around procedures
Radio procedures (various airspace)
Airspace navigation (using VOR/DME)
Power off stalls (only procedures, not the physical skills)
Power on stalls (only procedures, not the physical skills)
Positioning controls for wind during taxi
Side slipping on approach for crosswind (control inputs, not the actual landing)
Lost communications

LESSON 1: INDOCTRINATION

Lesson time: 0.5 hour

Objective: For the student to gain familiarization with aircraft control and instrument interpretation.

Content:

Functionality and use of primary flight controls
Functionality and use of primary engine controls
Functionality of the basic flight instruments
Operation of the engine controls and interpretation of the engine instruments
Use of elevator trim
Straight and level

- Relationship between pitch and airspeed/rate of climb
- Effects of changing power

Pre-maneuver checks (general)
Turns

- Attitude indicator
- Rate of turn and angle of bank
- Level turns

Completion Standards: Student is able to maintain flight within 400 feet altitude, 20 degrees of heading, and 20 knots while performing the maneuvers listed.

LESSON 2: PRIMARY FLIGHT SKILLS

Lesson time: 0.5 hour

Objective: For the student to learn and practice techniques for turning flight and slow flight. Emphasis will be on underlying principles and set-up of the maneuvers.

Content:

Pre-maneuver checks
Straight and level at target airspeeds
Level turns—10, 20, 30 degrees of bank

- Inclinometer—slips/skids
- Standard rate turns
- Turn coordination

- Shallow turns—explanation of adverse yaw, proper rudder technique
- Steeper turns—explanation of horizontal component of lift

Turns to a heading

Completion Standards: The student should be able to complete turns to within 20 degrees of a specified heading. During slow flight, student maintains altitude within 400 feet, heading within 20 degrees, airspeed with 20 knots.

LESSON 3: BASIC FLIGHT SKILLS—CONTINUED

Lesson time: 0.5 hour

Objective: For the student to combine previously learned skill sets and practice turns to headings while climbing/descending and leveling off.

Content:
Pre-maneuver checks (general)
Level-off techniques—climbs and descents
Constant airspeed climbs/descents to altitude
Constant rate climbs/descents to altitude
Climbing and descending turns to a heading and altitude
Slow flight

- Discussion of airplane performance with high induced drag
- Discussion of pitch and power use during the maneuver
- Maneuver set up
- Exploring performance at 60 knots (C172)
    - Climbs on heading
    - Descents on heading
    - Turns: climbing/descending/straight and level

Completion Standards: Upon completion the student should be able to complete turns to within 20 degrees of a specified heading, level off within 200 feet of altitude and maintain airspeed within 15 knots.

LESSON 4: INSTRUMENT SKILLS/ABNORMAL OPERATIONS

Lesson time: 0.5 hour

Objective: For the student to increase scanning proficiency and be introduced to instrument flying techniques. The student will also be introduced to unexpected instrument conditions including unusual attitudes.

Content:
Basic instrument skills—scanning techniques
Flying the numbers (pitch + power = performance)
Basic maneuvers
Abnormal operations

- Inadvertently encountering IMC
- Compass turns (and associated errors)
- Encountering turbulence
- Unusual attitude recovery
- Aborted takeoff—lack of indicated airspeed (ASI can be failed, or pitot tube blocked from the failures page—click setup/failures)

Completion Standards: Upon completion the student should be able to maintain altitude within 300 feet, heading within 15 degrees, and airspeed within 15 knots throughout maneuvering.

LESSON 5: EMERGENCIES AND EQUIPMENT MALFUNCTIONS

Lesson time: 0.5 hour

Objective: To introduce the student to various possible emergencies as well as their corresponding recovery actions.

Content:
Partial or complete power loss
Engine roughness or overheat
Loss of oil pressure
Fuel starvation
Electrical malfunction
Vacuum/pressure, and associated flight instruments malfunction
Pitot/static
Landing gear or flap malfunction
Inoperative trim
Structural icing
Smoke/fire/engine compartment fire
Any other emergency appropriate to the airplane

Completion Standards: Upon completion the student should have a grasp of the principles underlying the listed emergencies as well as their corrective actions.

LESSON 6: NAVIGATION

Lesson time: 0.5 hour

Objective: For the student to gain a practical understanding of radio navigation using the VOR and DME.

Content:

VOR introduction

- Components of VOR radio and display
- VOR navigation—concepts
    - o Demonstration—note: you can effectively demonstrate the principles of navigating with the VOR from On Top's position page (click setup/position) as well as from the map page (rewind/replay a flight to illustrate movement of the CDI.
    - o Course intercept
    - o Tracking

VOR exercises:

- Plotting a course using VOR radials (using sectional chart)
- VOR radio operation including identification and signal loss
- VOR intercept and tracking drills including station passage
- Dead reckoning
- Determining position (using sectional chart)

DME

Completion Standards: Upon completion the student should understand the principles of VOR navigation and DME. The student should be able to intercept and track a VOR radial while holding altitude within 300 feet, heading within 15 degrees, and airspeed within 10 knots.

LESSON 7: ADF NAVIGATION AND LOST PROCEDURES

Lesson time: 0.5 hour

Objective: For the student to understand the principles of radio navigation using ADF. The student will also learn how to proceed after becoming lost.

Content:

NDB and ADF

- Principle of bearings and ADF display
- Operating the ADF
- ADF relative bearing indicator (RBI)
- Orientation
- ADF exercises: homing drills

Lost procedures
- Initial actions
- Determining position with VOR/ADF
- Radio communications and radar services (using sectional chart)
- Navigating to an airport

Completion Standards: Upon completion the student should understand the principles of ADF radio navigation. The student should be able to home to an NDB station (or appropriate airport) using the ADF. Altitude should be within 300 feet, heading within 15 degrees and airspeed within 10 knots.

LESSON 8: CROSS-COUNTRY PROCEDURES

Lesson time: 0.5 hour

Objective: For the student to practice a pre-planned cross-country segment and become familiar with the associated elements, including radio work and dead reckoning. The student will also practice diverting.

Content:
Cross-country operations
- Obtaining weather
- Completion of planning, including Nav Log
- Cockpit organization
- Simulated flight segment
  1. Departure
  2. Communications, radio advisories and warnings
- ATIS and CTAF
- SIGMETS, AIRMETS, NOTAMS
- FSS communication—flight plans/flight plan changes
- Flight following
  3. Intercepting course (VOR radial) after takeoff
  4. Enroute—Completion of Nav Log
  5. Dead reckoning between points A and B
  6. Arrival procedures

Diversion
- Practicing unexpected diversion (using sectional)
- Alternate selection
- Estimate of heading, groundspeed, ETA and fuel

Completion Standards: Upon completion the student should be familiar with basic cross-country operations. The student should be able to track a VOR radial, know how to divert safely and know how to handle becoming lost. Altitude should be within 300 feet, heading within 15 degrees.

B

APPENDIX B: INSTRUMENT RATING PCATD SYLLABUS

The following lessons allow PCATD / Basic ATD technology to integrate with existing methods of aviation instruction and training. This syllabus follows the guidelines established in Advisory Circular 61-126, and can be used to reduce the total flight training hours, otherwise accomplished in an aircraft, needed to meet the requirements for an instrument rating under Part 61 or Part 141. Approved PCATDs or Basic ATDs may be used for not more than 10 hours of time that ordinarily would be acquired in an aircraft, a flight simulator, or flight training device. This syllabus also encourages using PCATDs or Basic ATDs to supplement the ground training and allows for 10 hours of time to replace the traditional classroom instructional techniques.

Instructors are encouraged to challenge students by altering the virtual environment within which the lessons take place. This can be done by changing the weather (adding turbulence, altering the winds, or assigning the ceiling and visibility to the approach minimum conditions) and/or simulating a system or engine failure. These changes can be set to occur randomly or within a specified time frame, allowing the students to learn flight and decision-making skills simultaneously. This method, in conjunction with training to the Practical Test Standards at all times, will encourage a willing suspension of disbelief and maximize the value of PCATDs or Basic ATDs used in a curriculum.

The following Modules may be supplemented using an approved PCATD/Basic ATD, in lieu of an aircraft for the flight training component, or traditional ground instruction for the ground training component. The following Modules are suggested because the associated tasks and placement within the curriculum lend themselves particularly well to an integrated flight training environment:

PCATD or Basic ATD Lesson	The Pilot's Manual: Instrument Rating Syllabus (ASA-PM-S-I)*	Time Logged
1	Stage 1, Module 1: Ground Training	1.0 hour
2	Stage 1, Module 2: Flight Training	1.0 hour
3	Stage 1, Module 3: Ground Training	1.0 hour
4	Stage 1, Module 4: Ground Training	1.0 hour
5	Stage 1, Module 4: Flight Training	1.0 hour
6	Stage 1, Module 5: Ground Training	1.5 hours
7	Stage 2, Module 2: Ground Training	1.0 hour

**This syllabus references The Pilot's Manual: Instrument Flying (#ASA-PM-3). The patterns listed in each Lesson's "Contents" can be found in Chapter 9 of the PM textbook.*

8	Stage 2, Module 2: Flight Training	1.0 hour
9	Stage 2, Module 3: Ground Training	1.0 hour
10	Stage 2, Module 3: Flight Training	1.0 hour
11	Stage 2, Module 4: Ground Training	1.0 hour
12	Stage 3, Module 1: Ground Training	1.5 hours
13	Stage 3, Module 1: Flight Training	1.5 hours
14	Stage 3, Module 3: Flight Training	1.0 hour
15	Stage 4, Module 1: Flight Training	1.5 hours
16	Stage 4, Module 2: Ground Training	1.0 hour
17	Stage 4, Module 3: Flight Training	1.0 hour
18	Stage 5, Module 4: Flight Training	1.0 hour

PCATD / LESSON 1

Minimum 141 Requirements: Dual, 1.0 hour PCATD/BATD

Objective: For the student to become familiar with PCATD / BATD features, and develop an understanding of instrument scanning techniques.

Content:

- PCATD / BATD orientation
  - o Physical controls
  - o Virtual controls
- Instrument cockpit check
- Instrument scanning technique
  - o Selective radial scan
  - o Basic T-scan
  - o Other scans

Assignment: *Instrument Flying*, Chapters 1 and 2

Completion Standards: The student must successfully complete all review questions following the assigned reading.

PCATD / LESSON 2

Minimum 141 Requirements: Dual, 1.0 hour PCATD/BATD

Objective: For the student to become proficient in flight by reference to instruments while maintaining changes of airspeed, and constant airspeed climbs and descents.

Content:

- Instrument scan
- Straight-and-level flight
- Standard rate turns
- Review effects of change of airspeed
- Constant airspeed climbs and descents
- Pattern B
- Pattern D
- Pattern G
- Review ground tracks

Assignment: *Instrument Flying*, Chapters 3 and 4

Completion Standards: The student must effectively control the airplane within 200 feet, 20 degrees, and 20 knots; perform standard rate turns; and successfully complete all review questions following the assigned reading.

PCATD / LESSON 3

Minimum 141 Requirements: Dual, 1.0 hour PCATD/BATD

Objective: For the student to gain understanding of the straight climb and descent, and turns, during instrument flight.

Content:

- The straight climb
  - o Climbing at different airspeeds
  - o Variations on entering the climb
  - o Climbing at a particular rate
- The straight descent
  - o Climbing away from a descent
  - o Descending at a particular rate
  - o The precision approach
- Turning
  - o Bank angle and rate of turn
  - o Roll-in and roll-out rate
  - o The medium level turn
  - o Instrument turns to a specific heading
  - o Climbing turns
  - o Descending turns
  - o Steep level turn
  - o Steep climbing turn
  - o Steep descending turn

  - Pattern A
  - Pattern H
  - Review ground tracks

Assignment: *Instrument Flying*, Chapters 5 and 6

Completion Standards: The student must successfully complete all review questions following the assigned reading, and effectively control the airplane within 200 feet, 20 degrees, and 20 knots, keeping all turns coordinated.

PCATD / LESSON 4

Minimum 141 Requirements: Dual, 1.0 hour PCATD/BATD

Objective: For the student to understand how to recognize and recover from unusual attitudes.

Content:

- Unusual attitudes
  - Recognizing an unusual attitude
  - Nose-low attitudes with increasing airspeed
  - Nose-high attitude with decreasing airspeed
  - Nose-high, and approaching the stall
- Pattern D
- Review ground tracks

Assignment: *Instrument Flying*, Chapter 7

Completion Standards: The student must successfully complete all review questions following the assigned reading; effectively control the airplane within 200 feet, 20 degrees, and 20 knots; and recover from unusual attitudes in a timely manner.

PCATD / LESSON 5

Minimum 141 Requirements: Dual, 1.0 hour PCATD/BATD

Objective: For the student to become proficient at performing timed turns to magnetic compass headings, and at constant-rate climbs and descents, flying solely by reference to instruments.

Content:

- Standard rate turns
- Steep turns
- Time turns to magnetic compass headings

- Pattern A
- Pattern C
- Review ground tracks

Assignment: *Instrument Flying*, Chapter 8

Completion Standards: This lesson is complete when the student can maintain flight within 150 feet, 15 degrees, and 15 knots, and successfully complete all review questions following the assigned reading.

PCATD / LESSON 6

Minimum 141 Requirements: Dual, 1.0 hour PCATD/BATD

Objective: For the student to gain understanding of normal instrument flight on a partial panel, and continue performing instrument flight training patterns.

Content:

- System failures
    - o Loss of heading and/or attitude indicators
- Interpreting pitch attitude on a partial panel
- Interpreting bank attitude on a partial panel
- Straight-and-level flight on a partial panel
- Climbing on a partial panel
- Descending on a partial panel
- Turning on a partial panel
- Recovery from unusual attitudes on a partial panel
- Seven Ts
- Performance sheet
- Pattern E
- Pattern F
- Review ground tracks

Assignment: *Instrument Flying*, Chapters 9 and 10

Completion Standards: The student must successfully complete all review questions following the assigned reading, and maintain flight within 150 feet, 15 degrees, and 15 knots, keeping all turns coordinated.

PCATD / LESSON 7

Minimum 141 Requirements: Dual, 1.0 hour PCATD/BATD

Objective: For the student to gain operational understanding of DME and the VOR.

Content:

DME

- o DME measures slant distance
- o DME uses the principle of secondary radar
- o DME frequencies
- o VOR/DME pairing
- o ILS/DME pairing
- o DME arcs

VOR

- o VOR radial
- o How the VOR works
- o The range of a VOR
- o VORs on aeronautical charts
- o VOR/DME, TACAN, VORTAC
- o VOR cockpit instrument
- o TO or FROM
- o Preparing the OBI for use
- o Orientation using the VOR
- o Tracking using the VOR
- o Intercepting a course using the VOR
- o The VOR instrument approach

- Pattern L
- Review ground tracks

Assignment: *Instrument Flying*, Chapter 14

Completion Standards: The student must successfully complete all review questions following the assigned reading, and maintain flight within 150 feet, 15 degrees, and 15 knots, keeping all turns coordinated.

PCATD / LESSON 8

Minimum 141 Requirements: Dual, 1.0 hour PCATD/BATD

Objective: For the student to become proficient at VOR navigation, and at intercepting and tracking VOR/VORTAC radials and DME arcs.

Content:

- VOR/VOT accuracy checks
- VOR navigation techniques
- Homing a VOR radial
- Intercepting and tracking VOR/VORTAC radials
- DME arcs

- VOR full approach
- Pattern J
- Review ground tracks

Assignment: *Instrument Flying*, Chapter 12

Completion Standards: The student must navigate using VORs, and intercept and track VOR/VORTAC radials and DME arcs. Flight should be maintained within 150 feet altitude, 15 knots airspeed, and 15 degrees heading, and the student must successfully complete all review questions following the assigned reading.

PCATD / LESSON 9

Minimum 141 Requirements: Dual, 1.0 hour PCATD/BATD

Objective: For the student to gain operational understanding of the NDB and ADF, the relative bearing indicator (RBI), the radio magnetic indicator (RMI), and the rotatable-card ADF.

Content:

- The NDB and ADF
    - o The Automatic Direction Finder
    - o The ADF Cockpit Display
- The Relative Bearing Indicator (RBI)
    - o Operational use of the RBI
    - o Tracking
    - o The NDB approach
- The Radio Magnetic Indicator (RMI) and Rotatable-card ADF
    - o Orientation using the RMI
    - o The initial interception of course
    - o Maintaining course
- Review ground tracks

Assignment: *Instrument Flying*, Chapter 11

Completion Standards: The student must successfully complete all review questions following the assigned reading, and maintain coordinated flight within 150 feet, 15 degrees, and 15 knots.

PCATD / LESSON 10

Minimum 141 Requirements: Dual, 1.0 hour PCATD/BATD

Objective: For the student to become familiar with radar, RNAV, and VHF direction finding, and become proficient with NDB navigation and intercepting and tracking NDB bearings.

Content:

- ADF orientation
- NDB navigation
- Homing with an NDB
- Tracking with an NDB
- Intercepting NDB bearings
- NDB full approach
- Radar
- RNAV
- VHF direction finding
- Review ground tracks

Assignment: *Instrument Flying*, Chapters 10 and 15

Completion Standards: The student must navigate using the NDB, and intercept and track NDB bearings. Flight should be maintained within 150 feet altitude, 15 knots airspeed, and 15 degrees heading, and the student must successfully complete all review questions following the assigned reading.

PCATD / LESSON 11

Minimum 141 Requirements: Dual, 1.0 hour PCATD/BATD

Objective: For the student to gain operational understanding of the Instrument Landing System (ILS).

Content:

- Flying the localizer
- Flying the localizer with an HSI
- Flying the localizer backcourse
- Flying the glide slope
- Marker beacons
- Approach lights
- Precision instrument runway markings
- Inoperative ILS components
- ILS full approach
- Simultaneous approaches
- Wind shear on the approach
- Pattern K
- Review ground tracks

Assignment:
Instrument Flying, Chapter 13

Completion Standards: The student must successfully complete all review questions following the assigned reading, and maintain coordinated flight within 150 feet, 15 degrees, and 15 knots.

PCATD / LESSON 12

Minimum 141 Requirements: Dual, 1.0 hour PCATD/BATD

Objective: For the student to gain understanding of holding patterns, procedure turns, and DME arcs.

Content:

- Holding patterns
  - o Tracking
  - o Corrections for wind
  - o Entering a holding pattern
  - o Holding speeds
- Procedure turns
  - o The 45/180 degree procedure turn
  - o The 80/260 degree procedure turn
  - o The base or teardrop turn
  - o Positioning in a racetrack pattern
- DME arcs
- Pattern I
- Review ground tracks

Assignment: *Instrument Flying*, Chapter 28

Completion Standards: The student must successfully complete all review questions following the assigned reading, and maintain coordinated flight within 150 feet, 15 degrees, and 15 knots.

PCATD / LESSON 13

Minimum 141 Requirements: Dual, 1.0 hour PCATD/BATD

Objective: For the student to be become proficient with entries to holds, and holding at VORs.

Content:

- Holding instructions
- Perform 3 holds at a VOR
  - o Direct entry, standard turns
  - o Parallel entry, nonstandard turns
  - o Teardrop entry, standard turns

- VOR approach, radar vectors
- Review ground tracks

Assignment: *Instrument Flying*, Chapter 27

Completion Standards: The student must understand entries to holds, and perform a hold using a VOR. The student should maintain altitude within 150 feet, airspeed within 15 knots, and heading within 15 degrees, and complete all review questions following the assigned reading.

PCATD / LESSON 14

Minimum 141 Requirements: Dual, 1.0 hour PCATD/BATD

Objective: For the student to become proficient in performing holds at an NDB.

Content:

- Perform NDB hold, standard and nonstandard turns
- Perform NDB hold, partial panel
- Review VOR holding procedures
- Intersection holding
- NDB full approach
- Review ground tracks

Assignment: *Instrument Flying*, Chapter 28

Completion Standards: The student must perform holds at an NDB using the correct entry and timing procedures, and maintain orientation at all times. The student must maintain altitude within 150 feet, airspeed within 15 knots, and heading within 15 degrees, and complete all review questions following the assigned reading.

PCATD / LESSON 15

Minimum 141 Requirements: Dual, 1.0 hour PCATD/BATD

Objective: For the student to become proficient in performing VOR approaches—full, radar vectors, straight-in and missed approach techniques.

Content:

- Full VOR approach
- VOR missed approach
- Radar vectors VOR approach, using straight-in minimums

- Partial panel VOR radar vectors approach
- Partial panel VOR missed approach
- Review ground tracks

Assignment: *Instrument Flying*, Chapter 29

Completion Standards: The student must perform VOR approaches (full, radar vectors, straight-in, missed approach) within 100 feet of altitude, and 3 dots of the CDI needle. The student must comply with ATC/instructor clearances, perform all procedures according to the approach plates, and successfully complete all review questions following the assigned reading.

PCATD / LESSON 16

Minimum 141 Requirements: Dual, 1.0 hour PCATD/BATD

Objective: For the student to become proficient in performing NDB approaches, demonstrating full, radar vectors, straight-in, and missed approach techniques, and be introduced to instrument departure procedures.

Content:
- DPs
- NDB full approach
- NDB missed approach
- NDB radar vector approach, using straight-in minimums
- NDB partial panel, radar vector approach
- NDB partial panel missed approach
- Review ground tracks

Assignment: *Instrument Flying*, Chapter 26

Completion Standards: The student must perform NDB full, radar vectors, missed, and straight-in approaches while maintaining flight within 100 feet above minimum descent altitude, not descending lower until a decision to land has been made. The student must maintain the flight within 10 degrees of the runway at the missed approach point. Student should complete all review questions following the assigned reading.

PCATD / LESSON 17

Minimum 141 Requirements: Dual, 1.0 hour PCATD/BATD

Objective: For the student to become proficient in performing ILS and localizer approaches, including missed approach, full and radar vector techniques.

Content:

- ILS full approach
- ILS missed approach
- ILS radar vector approach, using straight-in minimums
- Localizer radar vector approach
- Localizer back course full approach
- Localizer missed approach
- Review ground tracks

Assignment: *Instrument Flying*, Chapter 25

Completion Standards: The student must perform ILS full and radar vector approaches, and localizer approaches without descending below the minimum altitudes; maintain airspeed within 10 knots of approach speed; and arrive at the MDA prior to the MAP and perform a prompt missed approach at the accurate time. ILS approach must maintain glide slope within less than full needle deflection, and student must complete all review questions following the assigned reading.

PCATD / LESSON 18

Minimum 141 Requirements: Dual, 1.0 hour PCATD/BATD

Objective: For the student to practice instrument procedures in preparation for the checkride.

Content:

- Departure procedures
- Navigation to airway
- Steep turns
- Recovery from unusual attitudes
- VOR holding
- ADF holding (partial panel)
- Systems and equipment malfunctions
- VOR full approach (partial panel)
- NDB full approach
- Missed approach procedures
- ILS radar vectors approach
- Review ground tracks

Assignment: Instrument Practical Test Standards

Completion Standards: The student must perform all instrument procedures within Practical Test Standards and within specified minimums.

GLOSSARY

advanced ATD (AATD). An FAA-approved loggable desktop flight simulator, used with an enclosure and defined hardware equipment. Provides a training platform for both procedural and operational performance tasks related to ground and flight training towards a private pilot, commercial pilot, and airline transport pilot certificates, a flight instructor certificate, and instrument rating per 14 CFR parts 61 and 141.

artificial horizon. A flight instrument that provides the pilot with a visual reference when the natural horizon is not visible. A bar or display, held in a constant relationship with the earth's horizon by a gyro, serves as the reference.

basic aviation training device (basic ATD). An FAA-approved loggable desktop flight simulator used with hardware equipment. Provides a training platform for at least the procedural aspects of flight relating to an integrated ground and flight instrument training curriculum.

CFII. An instrument-rated flight instructor, authorized to provide instrument training.

control and performance concept. A method of attitude instrument flying in which one instrument is used for making attitude changes, and the other instruments are used to monitor the progress of the change.

currency. Meeting the legal requirements to exercise the pilot certificate, usually requiring a certain number of hours of flight time over a given period of time.

decision-making skills. The ability to use judgment in solving realistic problems, allowing pilots to control risk and ensure safety. Good decision making is measured by a pilot's consistent ability to keep himself/herself, any passengers, and the aircraft in good condition regardless of the conditions of any given flight.

deductive reasoning. A structured top-down analysis, used to identify the condition or event.

desktop flight simulator. A computer-driven software that duplicates the flight characteristics of an aircraft, typically working with hardware peripherals to control (fly) the aircraft. The simulator looks like the flight deck or cockpit of a specific aircraft. All the controls and instruments are computer driven, and they duplicate those in the aircraft. The controls have the same feel, and the instruments give the same indications as those in the real aircraft.

FAA-Industry Training Standards (FITS). A program focused on the technically advanced small reciprocating and jet-powered aircraft, introduced due to the recognition that the rapid introduction of new systems and technologies may not fit into existing training programs.

flight training device (FTD). A full-sized replica of the instruments, equipment, panels, and controls of an aircraft, or set of aircraft, in an open flight deck area or in an enclosed cockpit.

gauges. An instrument using an internal mechanism to show visually or aurally the attitude, altitude, or operation of an aircraft or aircraft part. It includes electronic devices for automatically controlling an aircraft in flight.

glass cockpit. An aircraft instrument system that uses a few multicolor cathode-ray-tube displays to replace a large number of mechanically actuated instruments.

instrument meteorological conditions (IMC). Weather conditions expressed in terms of visibility, distance from cloud, and ceiling less than the minimums specified for visual meteorological conditions (VMC).

MBT. Maneuvers-based training.

Multifunction Display (MFD). A liquid crystal or CRT display in a glass cockpit that combines primarily navigation, systems, and situational awareness information onto a single electronic display.

personal computer aviation training device (PCATD). A loggable device, using software that can be displayed on a personal computer and hardware (yoke, throttle quadrant, rudder pedals, and an avionics panel) to replicate the instrument panel of an airplane. A PCATD must replicate a type of airplane or family of airplanes and meet the FAA's virtual control requirements.

Primary Flight Display (PFD). A liquid crystal or CRT display in a glass cockpit that combines the primary six flight instruments plus other related navigation and situational awareness information into a single electronic display.

primary/supporting instruments. A method of attitude instrument flying using the instrument that provides the most direct indication of attitude and performance (primary instrument) in conjunction with the instrument(s) providing indirection indications of the aircraft attitude (supporting instrument).

proficiency. Competency in the area of operation appropriate to the airman certificate, rating, or authorization the pilot holds.

practical test standards (PTS). An FAA published list of standards that must be met for the issuance of a particular pilot certificate or rating. FAA inspectors and designated pilot examiners use these standards when conducting pilot practical tests and flight instructors should use the PTS while preparing applicants for practical tests.

risk management. The part of the decision making process which relies on situational awareness, problem recognition, and good judgment to reduce risks associated with each flight.

scanning. The first fundamental skill of instrument flight, also known as "cross-check"; the continuous and logical observation of instruments for attitude and performance information.

scenarios. A brief description of an event or a series of events, for the purpose of conveying a situation to evaluate in a training environment.

scenario-based training. A training system that uses highly structured scripts of "real-world" experiences to address flight-training objectives in an operational environment.

simulator. A device used for training or research that duplicates a piece of complex equipment. Flight simulators duplicate the cockpit of an airplane. All of the controls and instruments are connected to a computer that gives the operator the feel and the indications that would exist under actual flight conditions in a real aircraft. Emergency and unusual conditions can be simulated and practiced in the simulator far more safely and economically than can be done in the real aircraft.

single-pilot resource management (SRM). The "art and science" of managing all resources available to a single pilot to ensure the successful outcome of the flight.

situational awareness (or positional awareness). The accurate perception and understanding of all the factors and conditions within the four fundamental risk elements (pilot, aircraft, environment, and type of operation) that affect safety before, during, and after the flight.

spatial disorientation (SD). The state of confusion due to misleading information being sent to the brain from various sensory organs, resulting in a lack of awareness of the aircraft position in relation to a specific reference point.

technically advanced aircraft (TAA). A general aviation (GA) aircraft that contains a global positioning system (GPS) navigator with a moving map display, plus any additional systems. Traditional systems such as autopilots are included when combined with GPS navigators. This includes aircraft used in both VFR and IFR operations, with systems certified to either VFR or IFR standards.

visual meteorological conditions (VMC). 1) Meteorological conditions expressed in terms of visibility, distance from cloud, and ceiling meeting or exceeding the minimums specified for VFR. 2) Meteorological conditions expressed in terms of visibility, distance from cloud, and ceiling equal to or better than specified minima.

INDEX

ABOUT THE AUTHOR

Tom Gilmore is a full time flight instructor and owner/operator of Gilmore Aviation Services, engaged in advanced flight training (including advanced IFR, multi-engine, commercial and CFI training). Tom developed special training courses for this business, and is an Orlando FAAST team representative active in FAA Wings program, as well as president of the Stuart Chapter of the Florida Aero Club. Tom also conducts monthly aviation safety meetings and is an active supporter of the Witham Airport in Stuart, Florida.

Tom's licenses include Commercial, Instrument, Multiengine, Seaplane, CFIA&I&ME, AGI, IGI; he is a Gold Seal Flight Instructor and MCFI, has over 12,000 hours logged, and has been a flight instructor for over 37 years. He has written articles for NAFI Mentor, IFR and IFR Refresher, and contributes articles to the Florida Aero Club monthly newsletter.